Making Workers

Radical Geography

Series Editors:
Kate Derickson, Danny Dorling
and Jenny Pickerill

Also available:

In Their Place
The Imagined Geographies of Poverty
Stephen Crossley

Space Invaders
Radical Geographies of Protest
Paul Routledge

Making Workers

Radical Geographies
of Education

Katharyne Mitchell

PLUTO PRESS

First published 2018 by Pluto Press
345 Archway Road, London N6 5AA

www.plutobooks.com

Copyright © Katharyne Mitchell 2018

The right of Katharyne Mitchell to be identified as the author of this work
has been asserted by her in accordance with the Copyright, Designs and
Patents Act 1988.

British Library Cataloguing in Publication Data
A catalogue record for this book is available from the British Library

ISBN 978 0 7453 9987 4 Hardback
ISBN 978 0 7453 9985 0 Paperback
ISBN 978 1 7868 0132 6 PDF eBook
ISBN 978 1 7868 0134 0 Kindle eBook
ISBN 978 1 7868 0133 3 EPUB eBook

This book is printed on paper suitable for recycling and made from fully
managed and sustained forest sources. Logging, pulping and manufacturing
processes are expected to conform to the environmental standards of the
country of origin.

Typeset by Stanford DTP Services, Northampton, England

Simultaneously printed in the United Kingdom and United States of America

Contents

Acknowledgments

This is a project that spans two decades and that has involved many friends, students, and colleagues along the way. Some sections are adapted from earlier ideas and articles, and some of the initial writing was done in collaboration with others. Thus, first and foremost I want to acknowledge and thank my co-authors, who have generously allowed me to rework the articles we wrote together.

In Chapter 6 I adapted portions of an article written with Matt Sparke, whose luminous intelligence is reflected not just in this chapter but also throughout the entire manuscript. In Chapters 6 and 7 I also draw on articles co-authored with my former student Chris Lizotte, another brilliant thinker now on a postdoctoral fellowship at the University of Helsinki. Chris conducted the research in Chapter 6 on the Seattle Public Schools for his MA thesis at the University of Washington. In Part IV I have reworked two articles written with my former University of Washington colleague Sarah Elwood. The research that I draw on in this section was conducted jointly with Sarah, and additionally with the research assistance of three graduate students: Ryan Burns, Elyse Gordon, and Tricia Ruiz. I thank all of these individuals for their insights and comradeship at every stage of the mapping project. Two of the nine chapters were co-written with my research assistant Key MacFarlane, already a brilliant scholar in his own right.

The institutional support of several schools and programs enabled the research to go forward. These included Seattle Public Schools, Bellevue Public Schools, the Aki Kurose Middle School, the YMCA afterschool program, and Seattle Girls' School. Particular thanks go to the inspirational teachers Wendy Ewbank and Jerda Smeltzer.

The following foundations provided critical research support: the Spencer Foundation (several grants, including #20100052); the National Geographic Education Foundation (grant #2008-UI03), the John D. and Catherine T. MacArthur Foundation, the Royalty Research Fund at the University of Washington, and the John Simon Guggenheim Memorial Foundation. I would also like to express my gratitude for the support of the Walter Chapin Simpson Center for the Humanities at the University

of Washington. The Simpson Center, under the inspired leadership of
Kathy Woodward, provided an important model of public scholarship
and community engagement that has influenced my research, writing,
and teaching for well over a decade.

I am grateful to reviewers at Pluto Press for helping me to refine my
first draft in multiple ways. Thanks especially to David Castle for seeing
the project through. Many thanks also to Tiffany Grobelski and Philip
Thomas for their fabulous copy-editing, and to Matt Sparke for reading
and commenting on several of the chapters.

Many wonderful friends, students, and colleagues have been an
important part of the research process over the years. These include:
Ryan Adams, Mona Atia, Lance Bennett, Stefano Bettani, Ryan Burns,
Megan Carney, Ana Mari Cauce, Susan Craddock, Mona Domosh, Sarah
Elwood, Maria Fannin, Mónica Farías, Banu Gökariksel, Ricardo Gomez,
Elyse Gordon, Tiffany Grobelski, Jouni Häkli, Eleanor Hamilton, Gary
Hamilton, Rowan Hull-Bailey, Jennifer Hyndman, J.P. Jones, Susan
Joslyn, Kirsi Kallio, Cindi Katz, Sabine Lang, Helga Leitner, David Ley,
Chris Lizotte, Patricia Lopez, Key MacFarlane, Sallie Marston, Frances
McCue, Alison Mountz, Léonie Newhouse, Walter Parker, Jamie Peck,
Gerry Pratt, Ananya Roy, Tricia Ruiz, Eric Sheppard, Sheila Valencia,
Kathy Woodward, Henry Yeung, and Stephen Young. My greatest thanks
and love, as always, go to my family: Sage, Emma, and Matt.

Parts of the text of the present book have been adapted from earlier
publications, and I am grateful to the publishers for permission to use
them here:

Katharyne Mitchell, "Education for democratic citizenship: Transnationalism, multiculturalism, and the limits of liberalism," *Harvard
Educational Review* 71/1 (2001), pp. 51–78. Reprinted with
permission of Harvard Education Publishing Group.

Katharyne Mitchell, "Educating the national citizen in neoliberal
times: From the multicultural self to the strategic cosmopolitan,"
Transactions of the Institute of British Geographers 28/4 (2003),
pp. 387–403. Reprinted with permission of John Wiley & Sons.

Katharyne Mitchell, "Neoliberal governmentality in the European
Union: Education, training, and technologies of citizenship',
Environment and Planning D: Society and Space 24/2 (2006), pp.
389–407. Reprinted with permission of Sage Publishing.

Katharyne Mitchell and Sarah Elwood, "From redlining to benevolent societies: The emancipatory power of spatial thinking," *Theory and Research in Social Education* 40 (2012), pp. 134–163. Reprinted courtesy of Taylor & Francis.

Katharyne Mitchell and Sarah Elwood, "Intergenerational mapping and the cultural politics of memory," *Space and Polity* 17/1 (2013), pp. 33–52. Reprinted courtesy of Taylor & Francis.

Katharyne Mitchell and Chris Lizotte, "The grassroots and the gift: Moral authority, American philanthropy, and activism in education," *Foucault Studies* 18 (2014), pp. 66–89. Reprinted courtesy of Foucault Studies.

Katharyne Mitchell and Chris Lizotte, "Governing through failure: Neoliberalism, philanthropy and education reform in Seattle', in Michelle Brady and Randy Lippert (eds), *Neoliberal Governmentalities and the Ethnographic Imaginary*, Toronto: University of Toronto Press, 2016, pp. 221–244. Reprinted courtesy of University of Toronto Press.

Katharyne Mitchell and Matthew Sparke, "The New Washington consensus: Millennial philanthropy and the making of global market subjects," *Antipode* 48/3 (2016), pp. 724–749. Reprinted with permission of John Wiley & Sons.

Abbreviations

CES	Coalition for Essential Schools
CRPE	Center for Reinventing Public Education, University of Washington–Bothell
CTC	City Technology College
GIS	geographic information system
LLC	Lifelong Learning Credit
LLP	Lifelong Learning Plan
NCLB	No Child Left Behind Act 2001
NIDL	new international division of labor
OECD	Organisation for Economic Co-operation and Development
PPP	public–private partnership
RttT	Race to the Top
SPS	Seattle Public Schools
TNC	transnational corporation
UNESCO	United Nations Educational, Scientific and Cultural Organization

Series Preface

The Radical Geography series consists of accessible books which use geographical perspectives to understand issues of social and political concern. These short books include critiques of existing government policies and alternatives to staid ways of thinking about our societies. They feature stories of radical social and political activism, guides to achieving change, and arguments about why we need to think differently on many contemporary issues if we are to live better together on this planet.

A geographical perspective involves seeing the connections within and between places, as well as considering the role of space and scale to develop a new and better understanding of current problems. Written largely by academic geographers, books in the series deliberately target issues of political, environmental and social concern. The series showcases clear explications of geographical approaches to social problems, and it has a particular interest in action currently being undertaken to achieve positive change that is radical, achievable, real and relevant.

The target audience ranges from undergraduates to experienced scholars, as well as from activists to conventional policy-makers, but these books are also for people interested in the world who do not already have a radical outlook and who want to be engaged and informed by a short, well written and thought-provoking book.

Kate Derickson, Danny Dorling and Jenny Pickerill
Series Editors

PART I

Geographies of Work and Education

1

Spatial Divisions of Labor and the Search for Jobs

How do children become workers? In his classic ethnography, *Learning to Labor*, Paul Willis wrote about how the children of the working classes were constituted as manual laborers through various kinds of structural constraints, but also through their educational and personal choices, including their own agency and resistance in the classroom.[1]

These choices and associated forms of agency and resistance reflected the prevailing ideologies of work, masculinity, and community of that time period and place: England in the 1970s. Instead of focusing only on structural issues, Willis discerned how young men of the working classes—the "lads"—found respect, how they learned to value themselves. His focus thus turned to questions of culture, which he tied to those of political economy.

Culture has changed in the four decades since Willis's book was written—cultures of childhood as well as cultures of work and value. So has the actual workplace. So how are we valued by society and how do we value ourselves now? And what are the forces that are creating feelings of self and broader webs of belief?

We need to reexamine the types of questions Willis asked in light of contemporary changes in culture and society. How do kids "learn to labor" in ways that are both similar and different in the current moment? The contemporary period for young people almost everywhere is one of increasing precarity, where insecurities in the economy and labor market have been transferred onto workers, and ultimately onto children. Education prepares future workers for their entry into society—now a global society. The risks that young people are required to assume are thus global in scope, reflecting the flexibility and volatility of financial and labor markets without borders. They are also highly geographical, in the sense of a world unevenly developed, with deep rifts between cities, regions and nations, and with ongoing spatial divisions of opportunity and vulnerability.

In this context, what and how children are taught, and how and what they learn, can tell us a lot about both prevailing cultural norms and the political economy of the early twenty-first century. It can also tell us about how these norms are produced and contested. We need to know the overarching policy shifts and key struggles that are currently being waged in the name of educational and personal value. Who is weighing in on the content of the curriculum, the use of technology in the classroom, and on the types of schools and school choice that society should provide?

In this book I point to some of the new actors, technologies, and practices now being brought to bear on making children into workers. Beginning with a discussion of the shifting geographies of employment, I then move to examine how spatial changes in the opportunities of work, and the technologies that facilitate these shifts, also lead to new understandings of self and new cultural narratives and ways of being in the world.

I show that an influential actor in these processes today is philanthropy. The importance of philanthropic foundations is not just in their funding and programing priorities, but also in the ways in which they recruit young people and their parents into a new sense of value and security in vulnerable times. Much of this "value" resides in the opportunity to choose schools and learning styles, an opportunity that dovetails with market-based logics of individual free choice. This freedom entails certain kinds of responsibility and certain kinds of mobility—the right to be place-less rather than place-bound—an option for some, but not others.

I also look at regional, national, and supranational forms of educational governance over this same period. How have ideas about educating children to become democratic members of a diverse national community fused with and/or been displaced by something else? I examine ideas about multiculturalism in the context of labor market vulnerabilities, and contend that cultural ideas about work and its connection to multicultural education have shifted in this realm as well. Strategic ideas of cosmopolitan competence and lifelong learning now transcend those of social cohesion and national harmony. Here the watchword is flexibility: the ability to nimbly leap between skills and across spaces to capture the open position in the global economy. Once again, those who cannot make this leap are left behind, in place.

In this book I make an argument for the importance of geographical thinking in education. How children become workers is tied to these new/old divisions of labor and flexible work, as well as to cultures of self that echo the vulnerabilities of the global marketplace. Education reflects and reproduces these tensions, but it can also be a site of resistance. We are now at a critical juncture in educational theory and practice, where it is imperative not only to critique market-based logics and forms of recruitment, but also to consider the ways in which these orientations can be effectively resisted.

In the final two chapters of the book I consider the role of new geographies of radical thought and action in forming these spaces of resistance. These spatial practices can take many forms. Here I introduce two projects conducted with middle-school students in collaboration with Sarah Elwood, a geography professor at the University of Washington. One consists of finding and mapping alternative historical sites that were important for marginalized groups. They may have been neglected or deliberately overlooked in mainstream maps and tourist guides, so finding them and placing them on the students' own collaborative maps is a move that gives power to the children and also to the marginalized groups themselves. We call this project "counter-mapping" to indicate a refusal to abide by the normative rules of map-making.

A second project involves tracing the history and geography of a river. In this collective program the researchers worked with young people to find, map, and discuss the transformative relationship between humans and nature. Thinking and talking about straightening, dredging, damming, draining, polluting, and ultimately cleaning and caring for this "organic machine" is a project about the past and the future. It enables understanding about human and nonhuman relationships. It also helps children consider and imagine alternative future partnerships with each other and with the natural world.

The world of work is formed by geographical relationships and visions. It is composed of certain kinds of partnerships, involving humans and sometimes involving nonhumans as well. This world is one of uneven development and inequitable relationships and opportunities, an unevenness that reflects spatial production within a capitalist system. Abolishing these inequalities is thus also a geographical project, and one that must be considered at every scale, from the classroom to the globe.

This book takes on these scales of injustice, beginning with the global divisions of labor and ending with radical geographies of education. Each of the chapters draws on illustrative examples from research conducted in Canada, the United States, and England over the past two decades. My goal is not to provide a comprehensive analysis of these societies but rather to emphasize the geographical underpinnings of some of the key transformations now occurring in how children are educated and workers are made. I also hope to give some useful examples of radical geographies in action: pedagogies and practices of resistance that can form a broad bulwark against the fragmenting and dislocating forces of market-led globalization.

Geographers, especially those that study human dynamics, use the concepts of place, space, and scale to think about relationships between and across places. These heuristic tools lend themselves to critical, and even radical, perspectives to the degree that they force thinking about the uneven distribution of resources and access to sites of power and opportunity. In what follows I hope to introduce readers to some of the concepts most useful to radical geographers, beginning with the key concept of uneven development.

Uneven Development

What work is available is a geographical question. There has always been competition for jobs, but up until a few decades ago, this competition was largely restricted by national boundaries. We are now in a global marketplace, where workers compete for employment across borders. This contemporary story of competition in a borderless landscape is set within a larger history of uneven geographical development.

Uneven development is related to the logic of capital accumulation within a capitalist socioeconomic system. Capitalism reshapes the world through its inherent dynamism, and also through its own internal contradictions. The first of these involves the competition to reduce costs and increase profits through various ways of exploiting labor— for example, through longer workdays or speeding up the production process. This often leads to efforts by workers to protect themselves by forming unions or otherwise resisting these forms of labor exploitation. A useful way of describing this is in terms of labor "constituting itself as a class," a process that generally results in conflict between labor and business management. Because this overall process of labor exploitation and ensuing efforts at class-based forms of protection is fundamental to how the system works, and has worked historically, this is considered to be an inherent contradiction within capitalism.

The second major contradiction occurs when the production process actually works too well and excessive amounts of goods or commodities are produced. This is known as the tendency to "overaccumulation," where too many goods or too much capital is produced relative to the possibilities of its deployment. This is the direct result of individual competition between capitalists to produce more for less. This process often leads to a glut on the market, a falling rate of profit, and ultimately works to the detriment of capitalists' collective interests—hence it is a "contradiction" in the system as a whole.

The geographer David Harvey was one of the first scholars to make a strong connection between how capitalism operates in this dynamic but contradictory way, and how the built environment is transformed over time. He developed this thesis in his book *Limits to Capital* and other early work.[2] Harvey proposed a theory of uneven geographical development that drew explicitly on critiques of the workings of capitalism as developed primarily by Karl Marx. Among the many ways that he illuminated and expanded on Marx's critique of political economy, a key idea came to be known as the "spatial fix." This was the idea that crises of overaccumulation, such as discussed above, can be temporarily resolved through geographical expansion.

For example, investment in basic commodity production can build up to a crisis of overproduction. This overproduction leads to a superfluity of commodities that cannot be sold, and money, idle machinery, or unemployed labor that cannot be productively put to use. Harvey called this a crisis of overproduction in the "primary circuit" (the circuit of commodity production). He argued that a temporary "fix" to this crisis was to channel the excess into a secondary circuit: that of the built environment. Putting this excess capital, goods, and/or labor to work in producing urban infrastructure, office buildings, and housing "fixed" the problem of overaccumulation—on a temporary basis—by soaking up the unproductive capital and switching it into a new productive venue: the built environment.

While the intricacies of Harvey's arguments are beyond the scope of this book, his ideas are worth introducing because of the important connections he makes between capital, labor, and spatial production. Uneven spatial development stems from the logic of capital markets— of capitalism as a socio-economic system. The competition between individual capitalists, the tendency to create monopolies and to explore and exploit new markets, capitalism's own internal contradictions, and the tendency to crisis, all come together to create unequal capitalist spaces and environments, and inequitable labor opportunities.

Neil Smith and many others have developed this intellectual project further, showing how the entire natural world becomes capitalized and subject to new rounds of uneven development under capitalism.[3] The scale of this process is now global, and has fed into various regimes of imperial expansion throughout history. Challenging these iterative processes and effects must be first and foremost a geographical project as well as a social struggle.

Uneven geographical development today takes place at all scales, from pockets of extreme poverty in the financial centers of major cities to unequal relationships between nations and world regions. Who works where, in what kinds of jobs, and under what circumstances is directly linked with this larger process of uneven spatial development. The divisions of labor, from internal workplace divisions to international and digital divides, reflect these geographies of imperialism and capitalism. Moreover, contemporary divisions of labor continue to transform in new ways and in novel configurations, mirroring the spatiotemporal context of both capitalism and technological change.

The processes affecting the educational constitution of workers are global ones. The focus of this book is on the developed or core economies and societies of the anglophone West, with most examples derived from research in the United States, Canada, and England. It is an investigation of how workers are divided, educated, and "made" in these specific milieus within the global context of uneven geographical development. In this book I also take a look at how this social-geographical project can be reworked and reconstituted as something else—through geographical education, memory, and struggle. Before proceeding further, however, what exactly are the divisions that impact workers today, and from where have they emerged?

Capitalist Development and Spatial Divisions of Labor

The earliest divisions of labor within capitalist commodity production were in specific, individual factories. Rather than similar work being performed by all laborers on a whole project from beginning to end, work was divided into different parts and carried through in a series of steps. Each of the steps could be conducted by individual workers with different specializations, hence the labor process was seen to be "divided." Adam Smith famously wrote about this in *The Wealth of Nations,* in his illustration of the specialized manufacture of pins in a pin factory.[4]

The technical division of labor in a single factory from Smith's era (the mid-1700s) was the first of many iterations of this process. Each one was an attempt to increase productivity through revolutionizing the work process. The organization and constant reorganization of labor in this manner was made possible through the structure of social relations under capitalism. Laborers working for a wage could be directed and utilized as factors of production similar to any other factor.

Through the new social relations of production beginning at the time of Smith's pin factory, but greatly expanding during the industrial revolution, workers were forced to concede power over their spatial and technical skills and positions within the work process. It thus became possible to "divide" them in terms of their skill base, their tasks, their physical location in a factory, and their geographical location at all scales from city to globe. Technological changes from new machinery to the digital revolution have enabled these technical and geographical divisions within the labor process to take place.

The constant reorganization of production to take advantage of these multiple divisions has been one of the greatest means of increasing profitability since the advent of the capitalist system. A good recent example of this is the rise of call centers in India. These new telecommunication sites employ educated and experienced workers at far lower labor costs than is possible in developed countries, leading to greater overall profits for corporate headquarters.

One of the most prominent efforts to conceptualize and link the geography of employment to these social relations of production was made by Doreen Massey in *Spatial Divisions of Labor.*[5] Focusing on the more recent divisions of labor in the period of modern globalization of from the 1960s to the early 1980s, she explained how the spatial distribution of employment has to do with the way in which production is organized across space. She identified the emergence of new international divisions of labor, wherein the complex hierarchies of functions within capitalist production systems become stretched over space.

Massey's scholarship addressed contemporary divisions of labor that were themselves established on the basis of prior international relationships and patterns. These included the "old" international division of labor, where resources were extracted from the colonies and profit was made through the manufacturing process in core European cities such as Birmingham, Liverpool, and Manchester. In the industrial era, less developed regions of the world supplied primary resources such as minerals, cotton, and other basic goods to these metropolitan centers. These primary resources were then made into commodities in factories in the core countries, producing value domestically through the manufacturing process.

The decline of manufacturing in advanced economies and the spatial shift of these jobs to developing regions in the 1970s and 1980s transformed this prior pattern. The "new" international division of labor (NIDL) also involves a production process linking people and places across national borders. But in this case it is characterized by industrial decline in advanced economies and the rapid growth of manufacturing and export-oriented assembly plants around the world. While these factories were initially located primarily in border towns in Mexico and the coastal cities of Southeast Asia, they have now rapidly expanded to other regions such as Pakistan, Malaysia, and China. These factories are owned or contracted by multi-sited companies known as "transnational corporations" (TNCs) that coordinate the assembly and processing of parts and materials on a global scale. The resulting global production networks allow TNCs to play off different locations against one another, often forcing local governments and communities to accept lower tax rates, lower labor protections, and weakened regulatory oversight as the price for local jobs in global networks.

TNCs are generally headquartered in cities that are financially influential and also highly integrated in the global economy, such as New York, London, Shanghai, Paris, and Singapore. These so-called "global cities" are the key nodes of the production process, performing the command and control functions of management and overall system coordination. TNC executives search for the regions with the lowest costs in labor, land, taxes, and environmental regulations, and outsource parts of their business to these overseas locations. Thus value is created and profits extracted through a production process that literally extends around the world. Shifts in geographical production are directly related to the social relations of production, spatial unevenness, and hierarchies that enable TNCs to find and exploit sourcing efficiencies globally.

While the geography of the NIDL looks quite different from earlier eras, it still rests on and is made possible by social relations of production that enable the separation of workers and worker tasks into discrete parts. Transnational commodity chains involve a procedural or technical split in the production process—a so-called technical division of labor—in the same way that Smith noted for the pin factory. But they also increasingly involve a transnational political division of labor that—in a manner that often reworks the racialized divisions of labor of the colonial period—pits workers in different world regions against each other. Capitalist competition leads to the ceaseless reorganization of this process in the search for greater profitability, and technological innovations enable these transformations to occur.

The most recent geographical transformations of the division of labor—the development of global commodity chains—were made possible by multiple recent technological developments. A commodity chain is a shorthand way of describing the linked chain of places and events involving the initial drawing together of resources and production of a good all the way through to its eventual distribution and exchange in the marketplace. This process can now involve multiple sectors, players, and places across the globe. The technological innovations that facilitated this process over the past 50 years include telecommunications, containerized shipping, new forms of transportation including jet planes, and of course the revolution in computing and other digital technologies.

These new technologies have rendered the spaces of the globe easier to cross both physically and electronically, leading to the phenomenon known as "time–space compression." This is a geographical term meant to capture the ways that the temporal and spatial dimensions of the globe seem to be shrinking because of the ever-increasing speeds at which bodies and information are able to travel across space. Technologies have facilitated the acceleration of these processes in every conceivable way, from increasing the volume of goods, information, and bodies that can and have traversed space, to the speed at which these movements occur.

TNCs are the logical outgrowth of many of these processes and have grown enormously over the past four decades. They optimize the possibilities of the NIDL, restlessly searching for locations and workers that enable input costs to be lessened. They simultaneously probe for—and create—uneven geographies that can be exploited for maximum market penetration. These globalizing efficiencies and market quests have created rapid changes in where manufacturing occurs, how products are put together, and where and how products cross borders and are marketed to consumers.

For workers in core countries, the most widespread effect of TNCs' activities has been the offshoring of manufacturing. Many manufacturing jobs have been outsourced to developing countries, while the functions of research and development, producer services, and executive decision-making have remained primarily in the developed or core regions and cities. This process began in the late 1960s and accelerated through the 1980s, leading to what Bluestone and Harrison called, in the US context, "the de-industrialization of America."[6] The loss of certain kinds of blue-collar manufacturing jobs in the United States and most other advanced economies at this time was paralleled by the increase of low-skilled assembly-line jobs in many developing countries, often located in export zones along international borders.

These transformations occurred simultaneously with the rise of service-sector employment and other telecommuting and data-entry labor opportunities. A situation in which manufacturing declines, despite some growth in research, information, and services, is often termed a postindustrial economy. Initially, these "postindustrial" clerical and service-sector jobs grew most rapidly in developed countries, but in recent years this type of employment has now spread to other regions worldwide, such as India. Indeed, the call centers that first opened up in cities such as Delhi began as business operations outsourced from US-based companies like General Electric in the latter half of the 1980s. Now multiple cities across India offer IT services to TNCs across the globe, from tele-banking to tele-education and other communications operations. It has become more and more likely that the person answering a corporate call about a parking ticket, student loan, or airline dispute will be working in a cubicle in Mumbai or Bangalore.

These types of broad shifts are notable for the ramifications they have on social relations. Social divisions of labor include gendered divisions and divisions based on race and ethnicity, as well as class fractions. Many of the manufacturing jobs that were lost in advanced economies in the 1970s and 1980s were relatively high-wage, unionized jobs held predominantly by white men. Deindustrialization in core countries has been geographically varied, however. Some industries, especially low-wage branch plants and data-entry centers, opened up in suburban areas at the same time that steel and automotive plants were moving offshore.

Initially women were hired for many of these clerical and service positions in the United States and Europe. And in developing societies, women have been the primary workforce in the new assembly-line plants prevalent in export zones, such as along the Mexican border. While women have always worked, and labor markets have always been segregated by gender to various degrees, the entry of women into new forms of waged labor worldwide has been a marked characteristic of this particular transformation in the spatial division of labor.

Analyzing the specific articulations of industrial restructuring and gendered divisions of labor necessitates more fine-grained studies than are possible here. This is also the case for deindustrialization, capital restructuring, and the processes of racialization. But the larger global shifts are still important to consider even as we understand the imperative to look more closely at the social and economic geographies of individual places.

In every era, major transformations in work have occurred alongside technological innovations and shifts in the spatial organization of production. These transformations are constant and ongoing. From the earliest development of capitalism and incipient forms of globalization, there have been multiple transformations in the forms that capitalist accumulation has taken, production has been organized, and the labor market has functioned. These have also been accompanied by changes in the ways that people define and value work, and conceptualize their own relationship to it. Many of the most recent shifts in production and work have been captured under the label of neoliberalism, and it is to this concept that I now turn.

Neoliberalism, Globalization, and Work

In his book, *Introducing Globalization*, Matthew Sparke noted that neo-liberalism "names an approach to governing capitalism that emphasizes liberalizing markets and making market forces the basis of economic coordination, social distribution, and personal motivation."[7] This definition captures neoliberalism as an ideological project, a set of market-oriented practices and a project of governance with impacts on individual conceptions of self-worth and value. As a system of governance it is also notable for the strong repudiation of previous regimes of accumulation, most notably the welfare state liberalism associated with Fordism.

Fordism is the term often given to the period just before and after World War II, when—after great social upheaval and struggle—many nation-states adopted a more interventionist approach in the regulation of the economy. Numerous governments of the more advanced economies became involved in managing demand and attempting to coordinate the relationship between supply and demand through various economic and social policies. These strategies of government intervention extended to areas of worker rights such as systems of union arbitration and wage negotiations, with the overall intent being coordination and management of national economic development.

Government intervention also extended to systems of social reproduction, such as public housing, subsidized health care, welfare, and expanded opportunities in education. Related policies and developments included, for example, the G.I. Bill of 1944 in the United States—which, among other things, subsidized returning veterans to attend college. They also included the initiation of a unified National Health Service in the United Kingdom, and similar nationally organized health-care systems in Canada and France. Fordism took different forms in different nation-states, but at its height it involved, to some measure, most of the core, industrialized countries of Western Europe, North America and the southern hemisphere. As a whole, this regime of nationally coordinated management, development, and social protections has been labeled welfare state capitalism or Keynesianism, the latter term derived from the influential economist John Maynard Keynes.

The Fordist moment was relatively short-lived. It was succeeded by a regime characterized by the rollback of state protections and forms of social welfare, and the rollout of state efforts to facilitate business interests and market expansion.[8] This regime, often termed neo- or "new" liberalism, is characterized by an emphasis on freedom—freedom of the market and of individuals. This emphasis indicates a kind of return to the classical liberalism of John Locke and other early liberal philosophers, who advocated personal and business liberties unimpeded and unimpaired (in their view) by government intervention.[9]

While this "new" liberalism reflects older variants in many respects, it is different in some critical ways. These include the fact that neoliberalism followed the period of Fordism, which led many neoliberal policy makers to adopt a forceful repudiation of welfarism in theory as well as in practice. It also includes the context of contemporary globalization and new forms of capital and labor mobility. The repudiation of Keynesian ideas of social intervention combined with the acceleration of global flows, have exacerbated and deepened uneven development at both global and local scales—with a number of negative effects for workers.

As market-friendly neoliberal policies have been promoted at the national scale by many advanced industrial societies, they have been buttressed globally by a number of free trade agreements and organizations such as the North American Free Trade Agreement (NAFTA) between the United States, Canada, and Mexico, and the World Trade Organization (WTO), which currently oversees trade agreements between 164 countries. These types of free trade agreements facilitate the smooth flow of goods across international borders because they disallow what are perceived to be impediments to these flows. These impediments are conceptualized as local, regional, or national forms of support or protection for nationally produced goods—protections that are seen to bring an unfair advantage with respect to the free trade process. Constraints to the free flow of commodities include import taxes and other kinds of trade barriers, but also locally or nationally based subsidies and/or environmental or worker protections in the production process.

Despite the strong refrain of equity and fairness that characterizes most of the discussion around free trade agreements and organizations, historical evidence and empirical research suggests that these types of neoliberal policies operate mainly to the benefit of wealthier countries and the corporate and business elites within all of the countries involved. Moreover, they frequently have a negative impact on workers and the environment. I now provide a quick snapshot of some worker-related impacts of one of these prominent free trade agreements.

NAFTA, implemented in 1994, led to the loss of manufacturing jobs in Canada and the United States as industries moved parts of their production process to *maquiladoras* (export processing zones) in northern Mexico. This move was made primarily to take advantage of the cheaper cost of labor in Mexico, but also because of the lower cost of land, lower taxes, and less onerous environmental and health regulations. It is estimated that between 1994 and 2010, nearly 700,000 US manufacturing jobs were lost, although there were some gains in the retail sector, and some of those losses can probably be attributed to the 2008 financial crisis.[10] Meanwhile, those companies that kept their factories in the United States were able to suppress the wages of workers by threatening to relocate if unions were organized or demands made for higher wages or better work conditions.

Mexican workers were also affected negatively by NAFTA. Despite free trade rhetoric calling for the removal of all protections and subsidies for nationally produced goods, the United States continued to subsidize its agriculture industry, including through the 2002 Farm Bill. This meant that when NAFTA led to the removal of trade tariffs (including for agricultural products), US companies were able to produce and export corn to Mexico at far lower prices than Mexican farmers could match. Mexican subsidies to farmers had been greatly reduced during this same period, and those subsidies that were allocated by the government went primarily to the country's larger farms. The upshot of this was that small-scale Mexican farmers could not compete and over 2 million lost their farms and livelihoods.[11]

A final piece of the story links the world of financial liberalization to that of employment. Neoliberal ideology upholds market freedom of all kinds, including the freeing up of capital as well as commodities. Business-friendly neoliberal policies thus lay the ground for the smoother and easier movement of capital across borders. After NAFTA went into effect, the Mexican government removed the last national controls over the financial movement of capital and devalued the peso in order to attract direct foreign investment from the United States. This move was intended to galvanize Mexico's export-led growth strategy, a strategy that had been pushed on Mexico by US corporate interests hoping to gain from the free trade agreement. The peso's devaluation, however, led to a severe economic crisis, which contributed to the uprooting of small-scale farmers and workers. This led, in turn, to even greater migration to the low-skilled, poorly paid assembly-line manufacturing plants in the export platforms on the border.[12]

Thus, while the corporate elite of both countries benefited from the free flow of capital and commodities across the border that NAFTA was designed to encourage, labor in both the United States and Mexico was negatively impacted. This case study shows how these types of free trade policies exacerbate existing inequities and reproduce uneven development. Yet NAFTA is still hyped as a good example of the benefits of free trade by most media and most national politicians—including those in developed and developing economies as well as those from different political parties. From Clinton to Bush to Obama and from Zedillo to Fox to Calderón to Nieto, the ongoing positive evaluation of NAFTA remained strong. And even though the current US president, Donald Trump, campaigned on a platform that was highly critical of free trade agreements such as NAFTA, the conservative Congress, plus

Trump's own business leanings, make it unlikely that any major changes to the agreement will be forthcoming.

We can see here that neoliberal forms of governance can become entrenched both practically and discursively in ways that are often difficult to dislodge. At the national scale, inequitable geopolitical relationships become normalized through seemingly common-sense assertions such as the benefit of free trade for all. These types of neoliberal ideologies are promoted as offering nations a level playing field and the freedom to compete as equal players. Media pundits and authors such as Thomas Friedman constantly extol the benefits of free trade in creating fairer exchanges, heralding it as a way of creating a "flatter," and hence a more equal and level playing field.[13] In practice, however, neoliberal forms of capitalism both profit from and exacerbate existing spaces of uneven (*not* level) national development. These types of inequities can also be created and/or deepened as a result of free-market ideologies and policies at the urban scale.

Urban environments and residents often absorb the brunt of laws, policies and programs promoted and financed—or not financed—at the national scale. Under state-led forms of development in the United States during the Fordist era, for example, numerous federal policies designed to facilitate the movement of interstate goods, encourage suburban development, and aid homeownership were key factors in the abandonment and deterioration of inner city neighborhoods. These included the legislation and subsidization of highways through the National Defense and Interstate Highway Act and its successors, the availability of federally subsidized home mortgages to returning veterans (white only) for new homes, and changing tax codes that encouraged businesses to abandon older structures by giving greater tax benefits for the construction of new buildings on greenfield sites.

Along with other institutional actors such as banks, and in conjunction with widespread racism, these federal actions encouraged suburban-ization, white flight and urban disinvestment in the post World War II period—processes that aided a spiral of inner city decline with ongoing ramifications for cities and urban populations. Among other effects, state-funded schools in many metropolitan areas experienced rapidly declining resources with the loss of more affluent white residents and a stable tax base. African-American, Latino, and other minority groups were frequently excluded from the new suburban housing tracts through racial covenants restricting who could buy a home, as well as the inability to access financing because of racism in federal and private home loan programs and housing markets. Ultimately, minority populations became trapped in rapidly deteriorating urban environments, and the state schools of many major US cities became both poorer and even more highly segregated by race during the late 1960s.

Meanwhile, during the neoliberal era cities have also been greatly impacted by the policy pronouncements and practices at national and supranational scales of governance. For example, declining federal support to cities beginning in the mid-1970s, alongside national cutbacks in social services and an eroding tax base, forced mayors and other urban planners to adopt more competitive, entrepreneurial strategies to attract business and capital to their metropolitan areas.[14] Instead of seeing managing funds and providing services to city residents as the primary goal and logic of city governance, the mantra became one of adopting market-friendly policies. These policy platforms could be anything from reducing taxes for businesses willing to "stay," to giving tax incentives to businesses willing to "come," to providing the types of labor, infra-structural, and environmental conditions considered most desirable to corporations.

The negative consequences of these business-friendly entrepreneur-ial strategies have included greater urban socioeconomic inequality, social exclusion, and increased forms of marginalization based on race and class. A good example here is the city of Glasgow, often hailed as the United Kingdom's "renaissance" city of the late twentieth century. Research by Gordon MacLeod documents the political strategies of urban entrepreneurialism and place-based marketing heralded by city leaders in the 1980s and 1990s, which led to a major reinvention of both the landscape and the imagery of the city. However, MacLeod's research also shows how this rebirth came at a huge cost. The aggressive marketing strategy for the city primarily benefited an urban elite, and negatively impacted a wider citizenry who experienced increasing forms of displacement, greater socioeconomic marginalization, and more surveillance and monitoring.[15]

The move from a more managerial structure of governance to more entrepreneurial practices and ways of thinking also had a number of direct ramifications for education as well as for urban residents and spaces. In the United States, sharp competition between cities to attract and keep capital and businesses at the end of the twentieth century contributed to a rapid slide downward in terms of unionization levels, worker benefits, and funding support for many urban services and amenities. In addition to services such as public transportation, parks and museums, reductions in funding also hit the education sector, including city-based colleges and state universities.[16]

In New York City, for example, the City University of New York (CUNY), experienced drastic budget cuts in the 1970s that led ultimately to the imposition of tuition fees for the first time in its history. (It was founded in 1847 to provide higher education opportunities for the city's poor.) The tuition charges introduced in 1976 caused an immediate decline in enrollment from 250,000 to 180,000 the following year. Historians of the institution have noted, further, that these actions occurred soon after the university began an open admissions process that greatly increased the numbers of black and Latino students. Indeed, tuition was imposed in the first year that the freshmen class became predominantly non-white. This has led many radical activists to proclaim the ongoing struggles at CUNY over budget cuts and tuition costs as primarily "a civil rights struggle, not an argument over economics or fiscal policy."[17]

The decreases in government funding for systems of higher education that began in the mid-1970s accelerated sharply in the 1980s and have continued through the present. According to the National Income and Product Accounts of the United States, government funding for higher education declined by 40.2 percent between 1980 and 2011, and for some states, the decline was as high as 69.4 percent.[18] While government support declined, tuition fees rose markedly during the same period. Between 1980 and 2012 the average tuition cost at US community colleges increased by 164 percent, and for premier state universities by 247 percent.[19] The United Kingdom has also seen rapid increases in the cost of university tuition since fees were introduced in 1998. Similarly, over the past decade the cost of university education in Canada has increased by an average of 40 percent.[20]

Ironically, in the US case, the rapidly escalating cost of tuition at community colleges and universities is now paralleled by a push by mayors and other urban politicians and planners to attract knowledge-based workers to help advance cities' fortunes in the context of federal disinvestment, white flight, and industrial and financial decline. The supposed benefits of attracting a core of computer designers and programers, scientists, professors, engineers, artists, and other creative people to aid in successful urban growth was articulated most prominently by Richard Florida in his book *The Rise of the Creative Class*.[21] In this and subsequent work, he argued that cities able to attract and engage creative and innovative individuals would benefit enormously, as they would transition into successful postindustrial cities at the vanguard of emerging financial and high-tech economic regimes.

Hence a common refrain of contemporary urban politicians has become the imperative to produce the conditions in which the super-creative will be attracted to come and live in the city. At the same time, the opportunities that might help produce these creative actors—such as affordable higher education—are increasingly inadequately funded. These urban policy prescriptions, formulated along the lines of the "creative city" thesis, are clearly designed for those who are already highly educated and/or have unconstrained access to expensive colleges and universities. The policies thus tend to benefit wealthier and whiter segments of society far more than anyone else, and, as I explore more in Chapter 4, frequently lead to gentrification and even greater economic inequalities and forms of marginalization based on both class and race.

Glocalization and Worker Mobility

Processes of neoliberal globalization leave workers worldwide in increasingly precarious positions. This precarity is compounded by the loss of social safety nets that had been struggled for and created during the Fordist era. Among the many ways that these social protections are eroded, a key way is via scaling up various kinds of financial and other forms of control to global institutions and actors, while responsibility for administering austerity and policing compliance is simultaneously scaled down to the city level. This process, which is termed "glocaliza-tion" by geographers, is useful to identify because of its tendency to diminish the role of the nation-state in providing both a regulatory and a social provisioning function for the city and its workers.

In his book *The Neoliberal City*, Jason Hackworth traces the impact of glocalization processes on American cities.[22] He shows, for example, how the decrease in federal support and aid to cities in the 1970s and 1980s necessitated a rapid increase in private borrowing and municipal debt. Cities' increasing reliance on the private debt market made them beholden to global bond-rating agencies and their assessment of a city's fiscal health. These global institutions were thenceforth accorded a certain degree of power and influence over public figures and systems of urban governance. If urban projects, reforms, and other spending priorities were not perceived to be financially beneficial to investors and the fiscal health of a city, these institutional global actors had the power to lower a city's rating and consign it to economic free fall.

Glocalization has an immense impact on urban residents and workers because it links the fate of local spaces and institutions to these broader financial, political, and regulatory systems beyond their control, and often beyond the control of their democratically elected representatives. A good example in the United Kingdom is the city of London, which lost much of its local political power and autonomy following the 1979 election of Margaret Thatcher as the country's prime minister. Similar to Ronald Reagan in the United States and Helmut Kohl in Germany, Thatcher used her power at the national level to push a neoliberal vision of society at every scale of governance. Cities and populations that resisted unfettered market development and the evisceration of traditional worker rights and protections were undermined. At the same time, private investors and public–private partnerships were celebrated and abetted.

During Thatcher's first term in office, the Greater London Council (GLC), a locally elected administrative body with power over land-use decisions and some welfare service provisioning, was defunded and abolished. The GLC was led at the time by Ken Livingstone, a leftist member of the Labour Party who opposed Thatcher's vision of privatization, deregulation, and market-led development for the city. After its dissolution in 1986, the GLC's powers were devolved to boroughs and numerous public–private partnerships, and many of its assets were sold to private companies. Among these types of partnerships were so-called quasi-autonomous non-governmental organizations, commonly known as "quangos."

These quangos, such as the London Docklands Development Corporation, were often appointed and funded by central government, but had significant power and autonomy to buy, redevelop, privatize, and dispose of government land. In the case of the Docklands, this massive redevelopment scheme was greatly aided by the government's provision of infrastructure, the designation of the area as an 'enterprise zone', the declaration of nearby working class areas as "blighted," and by significant tax relief given to businesses involved in the project.[23] Overall, the redevelopment project, known as Canary Wharf, became a major financial center in the city and was instrumental in the rapid gentrification of the area and the displacement of poor and working class families, many of whom had lived and worked in surrounding neighborhoods for generations.

The United Kingdom's 2016 vote to exit from the European Union, a process known as Brexit, provides another example where decisions and policies made at non-local scales have a great impact on cities and urban residents. Londoners voted overwhelmingly to stay in the EU, but the national vote went the other way, buoyed largely by the preferences of older, white, and rural residents. Thus workers in London, where global mobility is often more imperative, were again put at a great disadvantage by policies decided on at a different scale of governance.

Additionally, the fate of the 2.2 million EU nationals now employed in the United Kingdom—most based in London—is now extremely precarious.[24] For workers like these, the potential of labor mobility, such as cross-border movements within the EU, is increasingly necessary in order to take advantage of rapid shifts in the global economy. But even those relatively skilled and experienced workers who *are* able to be mobile remain extraordinarily vulnerable to abrupt and often unexpected changes in the national and/or geopolitical landscape.

Despite some similarities vis-à-vis dislocations of scale, however, these two cases impacting London residents are in fact quite disparate. Many scholars have seen the Brexit vote, as well as the recent election of Donald Trump as president of the United States, as part of a broad backlash against the negative effects of neoliberal globalization by the poor and middle classes. This anger and resistance, however, has been combined with anti-immigrant and often white supremacist narratives fomented and encouraged by reactionary populists to further their own political ends. Moreover, in the US case, while the narrative may be one of paternalistic protection for those left out of the globalization game, the actual laws, policies, and people put in place by Trump and his followers work to the advantage of the affluent elite and to the detriment of many of those who voted for him.[25]

Intra-EU mobility is promoted through several types of programs that aid students and workers to cross borders for education and employment in different member states.[26] Labor mobility is also promoted by the governments of less developed countries. In the latter case, the encouragement to travel overseas for work tends to be targeted primarily at those who can send money back home. Money returned by migrants to their home countries, known as remittances, provides an enormous source of revenue for developing economies.[27] As a result, there is often strong state promotion of worker mobility and flexibility, including various kinds of national organizations aiding migrants who work overseas. At the same time, however, these national promotions conceal the many difficulties experienced by numerous people at the border and/ or in the workforce. Many potential members of the global workforce are either blocked from moving across international borders or are detained and constrained once inside state territories, often serving as a form of indentured workforce after arrival.[28]

In addition to nationality, gender and race play a critical role in who can be flexible and mobile, who is positioned as desirable workers, and what forms of employment are available to them and where. These differentiated forms of labor opportunities reflect specific spatialities of power.[29] While these opportunities vary depending on context, some structural similarities can be identified in a number of examples worldwide. Women from developing countries (such as Indonesia and the Philippines), for example, are more likely to be hired as domestic laborers and in the service and care industries, while men are more likely to be hired as operatives and in technology and construction. In general, those who are perceived as low-skilled and/or minorities are far more likely to be harassed and detained at borders and to be employed in so-called 3D jobs: dangerous, dirty, and difficult.[30]

New Labor and the Knowledge Economy

In developed countries and political institutions such as the EU, the government's frequent promotion of worker flexibility is paralleled by a strong push toward imagining new kinds of labor and ways of being a worker. It is part of the broader promise of the current and future knowledge economy—a promise contextualized within the contemporary neoliberal global economy. There is an implicit guarantee held out to societies around the world: with new forms of training and an orientation to knowledge as the key driver of the twenty-first century, nations and individuals can prosper. These forms of knowledge, moreover, must be continually extended and expanded. The compact involves the necessity of being flexible in education and training, and mobile, with willingness to move where the economy is hot and one's skills are sought.

In reality, however, it is not always possible to "cash in" on the knowledge economy, no matter how much education or lifelong learning one has accrued. The opportunities are simply no longer there, or they are accessible only to a very few. In their book *The Global Auction,* Brown, Lauder and Ashton call this "the opportunity trap."[31] As the NIDL took off in the 1970s and 1980s, it was assumed that research and development and other forms of expert knowledge would continue to be located in affluent nations. And wealthier nations did indeed edge out others initially with divisions of labor that were skewed to the highly skilled in core economies. But now those educated in the West and other wealthy countries are losing out to lower bids by fast-rising emerging economies with strong education sectors such as India, China, and Russia.

As before, technological innovations facilitate these geographical shifts in work. The latest technologies enable the most recent kind of spatial division of labor, those of "digital Taylorism," which "involves the translation of various forms of knowledge work into working knowledge that can be digitally distributed worldwide."[32] Now there is price competition for those with various kinds of clerical expertise, with highly skilled jobs going to the lowest bidder, just as they have for low-skilled workers for the past several decades.

In the context of digitally distributed knowledge work, neoliberal globalization and new technologies have altered the spatial divisions of labor and the structure of work and society once again. Along with these changes, the implicit promise that if you have a college education you will succeed in the knowledge economy is no longer valid. There is too much social congestion worldwide in the competition for white-collar, middle-class jobs. This is now true not just for the advanced economies but also increasingly for semi-developed nations as well.

Despite this, current prevailing ideologies still nudge young people and their parents toward certain kinds of assumptions about identity and value in the context of the bargain of the knowledge economy. This is reflected in childhood learning, competition for certain kinds of valued institutional resources, and in contemporary educational demands. In the next chapter I look at some of these prevailing ideologies and practices.

2

Creating the Entrepreneurial Child

The story of neoliberal globalization and new global divisions of labor is a story about the alteration of work and society under capitalism. What accompanies this transformation in work locations and practices are the cultural understandings of work itself. The forms of available employment—such as manufacturing jobs, service sector work, or high tech opportunities—reflects the movement of capital and labor around the globe. But how different types of employment are perceived and valued, or not valued, reflects the cultural values of a society.

As I noted in the previous chapter, neoliberalism is an ideological project and regulatory program as well as a set of market-oriented practices and policies. As a term it encompasses prevailing understandings about who we are, how society works, and how different institutions in society— such as education—should be managed. These webs of belief about how things operate, or should operate, and how people should behave are rationalities of governance. Governance is a broader conceptual term than the category of government, which is more spatially defined and static.

Governance is a useful way of thinking about the process of governing, one in which the behavior of individuals and groups is managed or conducted in a certain direction. Rather than a specific, defined method of organization—such as a state government—it refers more broadly to a general sphere of action—the ways that people can be governed through certain beliefs and values established within a broad set of institutional, familial, religious and other spaces. Another term for this that appears frequently in the scholarly literature is governmentality. Whereas we might think about local government or the national government as specific entities that make laws or provide rules and regulations and other tangible and transparent methods of managing behavior, governance or governmentality describes more general and wide-ranging "rationalities" of thought that guide our belief systems and hence our actions in often unconscious ways.

Liberal rationalities of governance, for example, emphasize individual freedom and a balanced, self-governing system. In societies underpinned by liberalism—such as the United States, United Kingdom, and Canada— the "norm" or normal assumptions about how institutions such as education should operate uphold the rights of individuals to pursue their own goals and desires in this arena. This assumption of individual rights is often defined and set against a system of government that is perceived as forever encroaching on those freedoms.

Neoliberal governmentality maintains these liberal emphases but also reflects a more concerted interest in the development of individuals as self-investing entrepreneurial beings. Neoliberalism is concerned with setting the "field of action" so that informed individuals can make accurate cost–benefit calculations in pursuit of their own goals and desires. In a neoliberal way of thinking, it is the government's responsibil- ity to incentivize the individual's natural tendency to be entrepreneurial, take strategic risks, and make calculated self-investments; and it is the individual's responsibility to take those risks and be accountable for his or her investment and consumption choices.

If we look at the impact of neoliberal rationalities of governance in education today, the first thing that becomes apparent is the increasing imperative to make educational choices of various kinds. Choice is a key component of neoliberalism because it rests on ideas of both individual freedom and individual responsibility—the freedom to choose one thing over another and also to be held accountable for that choice. It is also particularly central to neoliberal rationalities because in order for people to make good choices they must have both the expert knowledge needed to make optimal decisions and they must also be incentivized to do so. Moreover, the "choice" must be seen as one that will improve their cir- cumstances in some way; it must be entrepreneurial. In other words, individuals must be provided with the tools and knowledge to make strategic educational choices *and* the circumstances or context in which they feel both willing and obligated to make them.

As we saw in the previous chapter, globalization and new technologi- cal developments have altered the physical and spatial structure of work and the opportunities for employment in contemporary life. These are structural constraints that greatly limit the types of choices that people can make. But at the same time, how children are raised and educated, how they come to value their own labor, and how and why they become certain kinds of students and workers also reflects choices made on the basis of prevailing rationalities of governance. The geographies of global uneven development affect how much choice any given worker has, but nearly all individuals, to some extent, are recruited into specific beliefs about labor, employment, education, schools, and the value of work in the neoliberal era, and make choices on the basis of these assumptions.

The French philosopher Michel Foucault has been an important thinker bringing together these ideas of changing economic formations, shifting notions of self and value, and rationalities of governance under liberalism and neoliberalism.[1] Rather than believing abstract knowledge claims to be universal and neutral, as in the work of most philosophers preceding him (with the notable exception of Friedrich Nietzsche), Foucault saw them as both historically and geographically contingent, and also laden with power relations. Most of his life's work was spent documenting this intersection of knowledge and power in different institutional fields, including systems of medicine, criminal justice, mental health, and sexuality through the eighteenth and nineteenth centuries.

Foucault excavated the historical record of these fields for examples of changes in the ways that bodies, minds, and things were understood, categorized, and discussed through time. He argued that transformations in the conceptualization of scientific knowledge and expertise during this period were extremely important for the formation of subjectivity, or how people perceived themselves and the world around them. As different domains of knowledge—such as medicine and criminal justice—were brought to bear on individuals and populations, they created new spaces and rationalities of governing. In other words, with the creation and development of new disciplines of thought and fields of scientific knowledge and expertise, people could be encouraged to, and then, importantly, choose to, for example, submit their bodies to medical "experts." They would rely on expert advice in the newly established fields and then consent to be cured of what was perceived at the time as madness, ill health, criminality, or inappropriate forms of sexuality.

It is not difficult to point to the many times in which these fields of expertise situated individuals and populations in highly negative and oppressive ways based on the scientific beliefs that were then emerging. For example, in *The History of Sexuality*, Foucault documented how homosexuality became perceived as a perverse form of sexuality that needed to be scientifically analyzed, discussed, categorized, and disciplined. And in his "genealogies" such as *The Birth of the Clinic* and *Madness and Civilization*, he showed how new assumptions about sickness and health, and sanity and insanity, led to binary categorizations of human well-being or "normality," with frequently disastrous repercussions for those who were psychoanalyzed and medicalized during these periods.

Yet it is equally important to see how, in many situations, these interventions could be productive—for example, in leading to better health outcomes in certain circumstances. In this respect, individuals (at least those who were not institutionalized against their will) became governable not because they could not understand that they were being directed or managed vis-à-vis the control of their own bodies, but because they consented to these types of "expert" interventions for quite rational reasons in the context of the modern knowledge of the era. Thus these were choices freely made, but also constrained within very specific relations of power and liberal rationalities of mind, body, order, and life itself.

In his last lectures, published in *The Birth of Biopolitics*, Foucault traced the history of liberal practice from the eighteenth century through to the early expressions of neoliberalism in the Chicago School of the post-World War II period.[2] His main argument was that liberalism as a practice of government evolved in complex ways that are differentiated by time and place. Over the last two centuries, and particularly since World War II, liberal practices of government have comprised myriad interventions intended to enable, encourage, and guide markets to prosper, populations to be well managed, and individuals to calculate risks and rewards and to make optimum rational choices.

Foucault's theories are useful for thinking about education and the ways that workers, young people, and their parents are directed toward certain ideas and choices about schools, curricula, learning practices, and employment. In contemporary neoliberalism, the economic form of the market inundates the social world, such that many social relationships and communities are deeply impacted by the logic of rational entrepreneurial behavior. Economists such as Gary Becker have named the figure of this era *Homo economicus*, arguing that individuals whose lifeworlds are mediated by the market will behave in economically rational ways in order to optimize their human capital and life chances.[3]

As Foucault noted in his discussion of Chicago-style neoliberalism, the model of *Homo economicus* produces a very specific vantage point on labor, one in which workers should be seen and understood as active, choice-making economic subjects. Because the social world is mediated through economic rationalities, their labor is seen to be a form of capital. As active economic agents, they are both capable of and responsible for the development of their capital, or "human capital," in this regard. Personal and social value is predicated on success in this investment, an investment in the "enterprise of the self" as an economic unit. This is quite similar to Becker's argument, except that Foucault was more attuned to the ways in which these investments are always made within specific and contingent relations of power.

In the market-mediated, globalized context of today, acquiring greater knowledge and knowledge-based skills is generally considered to be a key method of developing one's human capital. Thus education, and especially higher education, is seen as a calculated step in providing the necessary value-added to the figure of *Homo economicus*. While everyone is free to invest or not in this form of self-development, the choice not to invest—to opt out—can have serious consequences. Since the social and economic structure of society exists primarily in relation to the market and its forms of calculation and assessment, the value of human capital is likewise measured in these terms.

Nicholas Rose, who has elaborated on many of Foucault's ideas, is often associated with the governmentality literature. In his book *Powers of Freedom*, Rose introduced the concept of "responsibilization" to highlight both the choice and the necessity of opting *in* to the responsibilities of individual choice, calculation, and self-development.[4] It is exactly these types of freedoms, he argued, that aid in the formation of new subjectivities and ways of being in the world. "Numbers, and the techniques of calculation in terms of numbers," Rose wrote, "have a role in subjectification—they turn the individual into a calculating self endowed with a range of ways of thinking about, calculating about, predicting and judging their own activities and those of others."[5]

On a personal scale, these forms of calculation, assessment, and self-improvement exist in multiple spheres. In education we can see how individuals attempt to produce the conditions in which they can thrive and succeed. These involve efforts by parents to fashion schools and educational systems that they believe will enable their child to excel. They involve attempts by adults to learn and relearn the skills that will bring them advantages in employment.

However, the constant imperative to care for and improve oneself through self-investment is a freedom that exists in relation to the freedom and self-care of others. The development of personal human capital through education, for example, exists in relation to competing visions and implementations. Lifelong learning, which is frequently promoted as a quest for personal fulfillment is, at the same time, a quest for a leg up in relation to the other myriad workers with similar qualifications who are competing for the same job. Moreover, the more general pursuit of advantage in constructing a knowledge economy or creative city, discussed further in Chapter 4, is always at the same time a pursuit for comparative advantage in the regional, urban, or educational marketplace—a market that operates not on the so-called level playing field as celebrated by the media pundit Thomas Friedman, but rather one that reflects the uneven geographies of previous rounds of capitalist accumulation.[6]

This fundamental geographical unevenness of access to educational capital, as well as health citizenship and the myriad other ways in which human beings are expected to be responsible for their own development, is not always addressed adequately by governmentality scholars. Rose and Novas, among others, have been critiqued for focusing on the responsibilized self-management of wealthy biological citizens, neglecting how these projects of self-care are made possible by the inequitable power relations between the global North and South.[7] Sparke has noted, for example, how the medical calculations made by individuals in wealthy societies incorporate the lessons of medical experiments and other sources of bio-information from poor patients and experimental subjects located primarily in poor countries. Further, with contemporary austerity measures consuming the health budgets of these societies, the more general possibilities of biomedical advances and health management recede ever further into the distance for the poor everywhere—reducing health rights and access to health services even further.[8]

Rose and Novas's vision of responsible care for one's own human capital is premised on historical and geographical forms of differentiation—often stemming from colonialism. When and where someone is born greatly impacts the extent to which that person is able to successfully opt in to the responsibilities of individual choice, calculation, and self-development. Thus, knowing where someone or something is located—the physical, spatial position of an individual subject position—is critical because it can help to determine the specific ways in which technologies of governance operate, and how they succeed or fail.

Foucault's empirical work focused on European societies, and the specific discourses that he identified as productive of modern subjectivities were geographically specific to the West. This book also focuses primarily on the advanced Western societies of the United States, United Kingdom, and Canada. However, owing to some of the effects of globalization, many of Foucault's ideas about individual self-worth and the necessity of personal investment and constant self-improvement now have increasing resonance with many contemporary beliefs about education and the development of human capital worldwide.

Ethnographic studies from countries and populations as diverse as those in India, China, and Sudan have documented how youth in these societies are becoming increasingly oriented toward more market-oriented understandings of human capital and self-worth from a very young age. In India, Jeffrey, Jeffery, and Jeffery have noted how signs along the road to Delhi now advertise educational "institutions dedicated to 'giving your kids a head start in life' and multiple nurseries tailored to 'the exceptionally gifted child.'"[9] In China, Anagnost has described the growing discourse of *suzhi*, or the notion of value and quality, which has, in recent years, begun to "encompass the minute social distinctions defining a 'person of quality' in practices of consumption and the incitement of a middle-class desire for social mobility."[10] Likewise, in a longitudinal study spanning more than two decades, Cindi Katz has documented the changing ways that children in a Sudanese village are trained to optimize their life chances.[11] Owing to their own altered circumstances, these young people are now forced to engage the logic of entrepreneurialism and competition in a rapidly globalizing economy.

In a wider sense, these transformations toward more market-mediated logics indicate changes in both spaces and subjectivities. Adults do not suddenly become fully formed autonomous subjects with ideas about the necessity of making rational, productive choices as individually responsible actors. These kinds of subjectivities develop over the spaces of a lifetime. Thus in the next section I explore a few of the ways that strategies of child-rearing, the spaces of childhood, and the experiences of primary education systems in Western societies both reflect and help to reproduce assumptions about education, responsibility, and the development of human capital discussed above.

Changing Spaces and Strategies of Twenty-First Century Childhood

Over the past several decades both the strategies of child-rearing and the spaces in which children play have changed considerably. Here I consider the changing nature of children's geographies in the United States, but similar processes are evident globally. Large-scale and rapid urban development has claimed the few remaining open spaces of most major cities, and the old vacant lots and under-used parking areas in which young people once had the opportunity to initiate a ball game on their own have largely disappeared. Even more significant has been the precipitous decline in funding for public spaces and commonly held urban amenities. Federal aversion to providing fiscal aid to US cities, for example, was made infamous by the *New York Daily News* headline of October 30, 1975: "Ford to City: Drop Dead." This presidential antagonism towards the overall fiscal care of the city marked the beginning of the end of Keynesian-style interventions in urban life.

Although playing out differently across the country, the period of federal intervention in the social care and provision of resources to cities and urban residents came under increasingly sharp attack with the harsh roll back of the welfare state under President Reagan. Through the regimes of both Republicans and Democrats, the welfare to workfare mentality pushed the responsibility for social provisioning downward to corporations, states, city agencies, charities, and individuals. This financial devolution produced many negative repercussions for the play areas, health, and educational opportunities of children, particularly those living in poor neighborhoods.[12]

Disinvestment in the urban environment and in state-funded schools impacted poor and minority children most directly, often leading to shrinking spaces for play and for spatial mobility of any kind. As Katz noted for New York City, the local nature of children's lives means that "the disintegration of public funding for housing, schools, and neighborhood open spaces hits them harder than other urban dwellers."[13] Moreover, precipitated by the decline of disinvested neighborhoods and the growth of the so-called "rent gap" (the difference between land valuation and its potential profitability), gentrification accelerated through succeeding decades, appropriating many of the last remaining spaces in which impoverished youth felt safe and comfortable.

In addition to the push factor of declining vacant lots, playgrounds, and other open spaces, there was a simultaneous pull factor that began to keep many children closer to home. The discourse of "stranger danger"—the fear of unknown assailants—influenced a growing parental wish to keep children closely supervised. This fear increased with the highly sensationalized coverage of attacks on children that became standard media fare during the Reagan and Bush I regimes. Although statistics indicated that abuse and abduction by acquaintances and family members was (and remains) the highest cause of injury to children, many parents nevertheless reacted to the implied danger of violence from strangers by curtailing the movements and free play of their children in public spaces.[14]

Indeed, the culture shifted so rapidly during these decades that unsupervised children in public spaces began to be seen as something abnormal or even deviant. Parents who were oblivious of or resistant to these changing norms became increasingly at risk of state intervention in various forms. White parents who allowed their children to ride the subway or go to the park without an adult present could find the police called in and their parental values and rights under attack.[15] For the parents of minority children, the outcomes could be far worse. In the case of Tamir Rice, the twelve-year-old African-American boy brandishing a toy gun in a park in Cleveland, the outcome was death. The policeman who had been summoned waited less than two seconds after getting out of his car before gunning him down.[16]

For middle-class children, the loss of spatial freedom associated with the privatization and development of space and the fear of unknown assailants was accompanied by a loss of free time. A study by the Institute for Social Research at the University of Michigan showed, for example, that between 1981 and 1997, study time for children rose by almost 50 percent. This was paralleled by a marked increase in scheduled activities. As a result of these twin pressures, children experienced a decline of 12 hours per week of free time and a 50 percent drop in unstructured outdoor activities.[17]

One of the many casualties of the fear of strangers and loss of free time has been an increasing alienation from the natural world. This phenomenon led Richard Louv to diagnose the ills of modern American childhood with the phrase "nature deficit disorder." In his book *Last Child in the Woods,* he wrote about the many new limitations on environmental interactions that affected children during this time. These restrictions came at a cost, he argued, including shorter attention spans, greater risk of depression and obesity, and reduced respect and care for the natural environment.[18]

The physical loss of space, combined with parental fears and increasing pressures on time, led to the proliferation of new types of corporatized play spaces for young middle-class children starting in the late 1970s. A play-space industry developed in the United States with the introduction of eat-and-play type establishments such as Chuck E. Cheese's Pizza Time Theatre. In the 1980s, "soft contained play" equipment made its debut, opening the way for "pay for play" indoor entertainment centers such as Discovery Zone and the Leaps 'N' Bounds chain initially operated by McDonald's. These highly regulated and completely encapsulated spaces provided a padded, "injury-free" indoor space where children could release pent-up energy without ever having to step outside. They flourished briefly but then lost ground to more current play-space concepts, including children's edutainment centers.

Although the term "edutainment" initially described educationally oriented TV programs and CD-ROM games such as *Sesame Street* and *Blues Clues*, it is now frequently applied to location-based venues as well. The idea behind edutainment centers is to combine entertainment, active play, and learning in a contained environment. A typical edutainment complex has a current theme, such as Pirates of the Caribbean. In the course of visiting this type of play area, a child can move through different types of spaces at various speeds, choosing interesting-looking learning activities to engage with on his or her own. Thus two of the main contemporary parental concerns, safety and the productive use of time, are assuaged through the use of these corporate play spaces. But these highly structured spaces tend to delimit both imaginative, free-form play and child-initiated activities. Since most child-initiated activities generally involve a social component—as children often enlist friends, neighbors, or parents to join or watch their play activities—time spent in these corporate centers reduces social contact and orients the child to more individualized enrichment experiences.

Parents' increasing anxiety about competition and self-care, combined with the loss of public amenities and spaces for children, has created a context in which middle-class children are being directed towards productive pursuits in more and more highly regulated environments. Additionally, there are a myriad of other educationally productive activities designed for both active stimulation and to give children opportunities to self-improve and maximize their human capital. These include activities such as academic tutoring over the summer, athletic programs of all shapes and sizes, and of course lessons in every possible intellectually formative pursuit—from dance to music to art.

Indeed, for some parents, even the fetus is now expected to absorb culture in an intellectually productive manner. The so-called "Mozart effect" is an idea derived from a small study of college students that indicated that listening to certain kinds of music might enable greater powers of concentration and effectiveness in test-taking. This "effect" has been extended to babies, in the hope that playing this kind of music to them in the womb will stimulate their brains and make them smarter when they emerge to compete with other babies of the same age.

All of these productive pursuits for children are commercially marketed in what has become a recursive process. As parents become increasingly nervous about employment and life chances for themselves and their children, they are simultaneously bombarded with advertising about what they should do and buy so as to get ahead. Much of this is directed towards various kinds of human capital development, including toys and play equipment that reputedly has some educational value. Infants and children are no longer expected to just play; they must also learn and be productive in terms of their own lifelong learning and portfolio development.[19]

Ideally, for proponents of these toys, these two processes can occur at the same time. Attempts to combine playtime with accelerated brain development has become a multi-million dollar industry worldwide. A good example here is the development and marketing of Baby Einstein, a company that was founded by a stay-at-home mother in the late 1990s, later acquired by the Walt Disney Company in 2001 and Kids II, Inc. in 2013.

The premise of companies such as these is that certain kinds of interactive activities and products can promote language, skills, and other forms of infant development in a particularly effective manner. Not only are children expected to succeed with these learning props, they are projected to become the next Einstein—little geniuses in the making. The videos created for babies to watch include stories and music, but also careful product placement of certain kinds of "educational" toys. The overall effect thus includes a push towards the consumption of specific toys as well as particular ways of teaching and learning.

In addition to videos, such as Baby Beethoven and Baby Galileo, the Baby Einstein Company now includes so-called discovery kits. These include wild animal safari kits, Neptune's oceans kits, and multiple other ways that children can be safely yet productively stimulated. In practice these videos and kits mainly replicate—in a newly packaged and sophisticated format—the types of enriched learning experiences already experienced by most affluent children. But their great popularity manifests some of the latent anxieties even these dominant class fractions are experiencing in the new millennium.

One of the implicit promises of these types of edutainment products is that of exemplary achievement—of being ahead of the game, at the front of the pack, on top of the curve—all of the various metaphors for dominating and surpassing others. Indeed, early descriptions about the educational value of the Baby Einstein products implied superior cognitive development in a number of areas. These were removed from the website after complaints and adverse studies came out in the 2000s.[20] Regardless of the specific marketing employed, however, the overall impression given is the critical importance of building up the child's learning capacities from an extraordinarily young age. A parallel development is the fostering of a competitive undercurrent of advancement and success, one that is absorbed by parents, teachers, and children alike.

Within this context of privatization and conformance to an increasingly market-oriented society, there occurs a corresponding pressure to produce children who can perform well in this system. This is where the culture of child-rearing comes into the picture. The persistent valuation of a child's free time as productive or unproductive is a relatively new phenomenon, one clearly associated with the increasingly competitive drive to create high-performing adults and workers. In order to "succeed" in the market spaces of the global economy, children are now primed in countless ways. These include after-school and weekend lessons and activities as noted above, to the extent that many children experience no unscheduled time whatsoever and declining amounts of family time overall.

But this has not happened across the board. What has developed over the past few decades are strategies of child-rearing that are increasingly stratified by class. After a long-term participatory research project involving 88 families, sociologist Annette Lareau identified some major differences in middle-class and working-class methods of raising children. She named the new middle-class stress on productive learning "concerted cultivation."[21] This type of cultivation, she argued, exists in marked contrast with the child-rearing strategies of lower income parents, who place less emphasis on the deliberate grooming of their children for future entrepreneurial success. The difference is at least partly a function of economics, given that lessons and athletics programs are costly and require parental time and supervision. It is also related to increasingly divergent cultural attitudes.

Lareau's socioeconomic study indicated that the ideology of cultivation spawns and is spawned by a sense of entitlement and self-production that is creating new kinds of subjectivities in children and new orientations of youth toward adults. She found that in contrast with poorer families, children from middle-class environments are more prone to argue with their parents, be more competitive with and less caring towards siblings, and to retain a sense of privilege and individual rights that lead them to question and oppose authority figures. The children of poor and working-class families are more likely to be treated with direct parental authority rather than through negotiation, to play with and take care of siblings, and to have more opportunities to develop spaces of free play separate from adults.

Lareau contended that the concerted cultivation of middle-class children is part of a new era of hyper-parenting and over-scheduling in which the child is handled more and more like a product requiring daily manipulation and enhancement in order to elicit the best possible end result. The desired end result is not always obvious—even to parents themselves—but generally involves some combination of competitiveness and cosmopolitanism that has been unconsciously grafted from the marketplace to the youthful subject. This transference is not surprising, given that even the mission statements of many elementary schools now tout their prowess in educating six year olds for success in the global economy.

Thus the erstwhile spaces of childhood have substantially changed in the recent past, infiltrated by both material and ideological forces associated with the corporate world. Parents and children are increasingly oriented towards consumption, self-production, and a desire for the ongoing experience (and necessity) of individual enrichment. They have been made aware that they, and they alone, are accountable for maximizing their individual potential with flexibility and finesse in a rapidly changing environment. In this sense children are fast becoming the ultimate lifelong learners, responsible for their own perpetual self-mobilization and personal enhancement.

Consuming Schools and Curricula

Within the context of changing geographies of twenty-first-century education and the competitive need to get ahead, there is a growing consumer orientation to specific schools and curricula as well as to other educational products. Over the last few decades, one can chart a growing orientation towards certain types of educational systems and ideas that are thought to correspond to advancement and success in a competitive global education system and job market. Among these are programs with a strong technological focus as well as those that advertise success in the global economy, including gifted, bilingual, and/or "globally focused" primary schools and international high schools. The growing popularity of these latter types of schools indicates interest in academic success and potential business opportunities down the line. It also indicates a more generalized form of cosmopolitan capital that helps signify distinction from "local" or provincial students unable to access the productive prospects of contemporary globalization.

Dual language proficiency is seen here as both a form of human capital and as providing a competitive advantage. This includes a possible advantage in overall performance, since some studies indicate that students in immersion programs outpace their peers in other academic areas. The great irony, of course, is that historically in the United States and other immigrant societies, bilingualism is often seen in a negative light, especially when it is a resource held primarily by immigrants and their children. White nativist moves to promulgate English-only policies in the classroom (and workplace) still hold sway in many policy arenas, including laws barring non-English language teaching in state schools as recently as 2000 in Arizona and 2002 in Massachusetts. Nevertheless, when the advantages of bilingualism are seen as accessible to the white middle class, a different orientation emerges, in which the clear assets of linguistic competencies have produced a vocal subset of parents pushing dual-language programs.

In their edited book connecting bilingualism with the US labor market, Callahan and Gándara and their contributors have documented both the conflicting discourse of American bilingualism historically (and how it is bound up with questions of race and class, as well as cultural markers of status and identity), and also some of the new labor market pressures that are currently impacting the growth of dual-language education nationally. In most of the primary and secondary schools that have adopted bilingual strategies in the twenty-first century, there is a direct link made between language learning and students' economic futures with multinational corporations and/or in an international workplace. The editors put it bluntly: "The popularity of dual language programs for young students draws on the promise of bilingualism in preparation for a future in a global economy."[22]

In addition to success in the global economy, many schools also herald the importance of facilitating "lifelong learning" both in terms of language acquisition and the use of technology. The dual language John Stanford Elementary School in Seattle, for example, highlights the school's mission as creating "a culturally diverse community of life-long learners who demonstrate advanced skills in communication, international language and technology."[23]

In both these cases, the underpinning logic is one of implied comparative advantage, such that even at the level of primary school parents feel compelled to choose these types of technologically intensive and linguistically sophisticated programs for their children's ultimate success in the labor market. For secondary schools this orientation is even stronger, such that education scholars have named increasing calls for more and more international education (IE) or international baccalaureate high schools a new social movement in US state-funded education.

Walter Parker investigated this trend, noting that while international education movements and programs were heterogeneous, there was nevertheless a strong overarching discourse of national security with respect to both economic competitiveness and military preparedness.[24] Economic competitiveness was framed in terms of the challenges of globalization, particularly the fear that the United States was falling behind in relation to other nations in educating enterprising individuals. This was made particularly clear in a joint report by the National Academy of Science, the National Academy of Engineering, and the Institute of Medicine in 2005:

> Thanks to globalization, driven by modern communications and other advances, workers in virtually every sector must now face competitors who live just a mouse-click away in Ireland, Finland, China, India, or dozens of other nations whose economies are growing ... The committee is deeply concerned that the scientific and technological building blocks critical to our economic leadership are eroding at a time when many other nations are gathering strength.[25]

In many respects this urgent discourse of fear and dismay about falling behind in the global race is similar to an earlier drumbeat of state school failure from the 1983 report "A Nation at Risk."[26] Published during the Reagan era, this government report also blamed state education for failing to prepare students for the competitive world of the new global economy. In both situations, "expert" reports were created and disseminated. They were designed to promote anxiety about "failing" state schools and children's poor-quality education, reduce trust and respect in government systems and actors, and orient stakeholders to new experts and managers who can correct things.

Thirty-plus years later, however, one of the key differences to this rhetoric of failure is the additional way that parents themselves have been recruited into the position of education experts and managers. In earlier eras the narrative of state school failure, crisis, and salvation was internal to "experts." Today the responsibility for demanding, creating, and choosing better, more competitively successful schools has now been devolved to parents and families.

Of course the parental responsibility for choosing wisely is one that is specific to those who are educated enough and healthy enough to guide and nurture their offspring. The scrambling of the middle class to produce resilient subjects for the competitive global economy now eludes many lower-income members of the working class as well as the poor. This group now includes white, non-Hispanic Americans without high school (post-16) qualifications, whose risk of drug overdose, suicide, and alcohol-related mortality is at an all-time high.[27] For lower-income black families, the high rates of incarceration, especially for black males, renders these types of expert "choices" increasingly moot as well.[28]

For the middle classes, however, the entrepreneurial responsibility for demanding and choosing schools that will aid in successful student preparation for new forms of knowledge work in the global economy has greatly influenced parents and students. This is true for the choice of universities as well. As competitive pressures grow, students and parents increasingly set their sights on highly selective, brand-name institutions. This has occurred at the same time as the rapid increase in higher education tuition in the United States, as well as in the United Kingdom and Canada.

Changes in technology, such as online admissions processes and innovations such as the Common App in the United States, have facilitated applications and enabled individual students to apply to a greater number of institutions globally. Nevertheless, the reason that so many young people apply to so many universities is also bound up with the overwhelming pressure to find and attend the "best" possible school, both to access the most useful personal learning styles as well as future employment success.

Meanwhile, parental and student interest in attending an Ivy League university or other high-status anglophone college has gone global and is now marketed to aspiring students and parents worldwide. While the elite have pointed their children towards Oxford and Harvard for centuries, the preoccupation with highly selective, brand-name universities now extends to the new global middle class in greater numbers than ever before.

How to access these types of schools has become part of a billion dollar education industry, one that both produces and feeds parental anxieties about getting ahead in the competitive rat race that has become the higher education marketplace. For example, the 2002 book *Harvard Girl Liu Yiting* was a best-selling manual in China on how to educate and train one's child for acceptance at an Ivy League university.[29] It led to numerous similar books worldwide, as well as to a major increase of interest in and applications to highly selective universities in the United States and United Kingdom. For many universities, especially state-funded ones, the growing tuition fees from international students such as these has become essential for their survival. Now many colleges and universities in the West actively target and recruit these international students.[30]

One of the main suggestions in the book for parents hoping to raise academically successful children such as Liu was to engage in the types of "concerted cultivation" noted by Lareau in her study of middle-class child-rearing in the United States. These included emphasizing critical reasoning skills through argumentation with adults, character-building through physical exercises and skills, and cultural cosmopolitanism through travel and the expansion of intellectual horizons and opportunities.

These are all examples of now global efforts to gain a competitive advantage in the schooling of one's children and oneself. This effort is implicated in "concerted cultivation" strategies of child-rearing, as well as decisions around education—all the way up and down the ladder from day care to graduate school and from the intricacies of high-school math curricula to kindergarten afterschool programs. We can see this among many aspirants to the global knowledge economy despite increasing dislocations related to actual geographies of employment discussed in

Chapter 1. And, as colleges and universities become increasingly cash-strapped, the incentive to recruit and lure these aspirational students becomes a circular and self-fulfilling process.

In the current era of advanced neoliberal globalization, the process of responsibilization as outlined by Rose and others affects children and parents in myriad ways. Many of these are related to schooling and to what young people and their families are encouraged to demand and choose in the context of ever-greater forms of competition and entrepreneurial recruitment. Enlistment to new ways of thinking about education plays out in how ideas about freedom, choice, and success are portrayed. In the next three chapters I focus on shifts in the cultural values of schooling: what is seen to be useful in education in the context of global restructuring, by whom, and for what purposes.

PART II

Flexible Work, Strategic Workers

3

From Multicultural Citizen
to Global Businessman

In Part II, I investigate how assumptions about the importance of educating young people to be productive and patriotic citizens have shifted with the rise of neoliberal globalization. There is a geographical component to this. It starts with the observation that national systems of state-funded education in most advanced industrial societies were established and/or greatly expanded in the nineteenth century, when the nation-state was being consolidated and unified as a strong territorial and economic unit. Children, for the most part, were educated during this time in a national system that was understood to be spatially defined and territorially discrete, even as it sought to expand its international or imperial reach.

With contemporary forms of globalization and transnationalism, this era of national spatial consolidation has changed. With neoliberal restructuring, the state has shifted from a more regulatory role of national systems and industries towards the promotion of entrepreneurial strategies, flexible jobs and skills, and global partnerships. In this context it is useful to consider how supranational, national, regional, and local scales of government have become involved in promoting new ways of thinking about education and what it should accomplish. Chapters 4 and 5 address the promotion of philosophies such as lifelong learning and new struggles over educating children for global citizenship, while this chapter focuses on the shifting discourse of multiculturalism.

I look specifically at how, over the last few decades, there has been a subtle but intensifying shift from the constitution of a multicultural citizen directed toward personal and national development to the creation of a more entrepreneurial, globally oriented businessperson. This figure is motivated less by ideals of national unity in diversity than by assumptions of global competitiveness and the necessity to be entrepreneurial and to strategically adapt—as *Homo economicus*—to rapidly shifting personal and international contexts.

The changes promoted in the philosophy and practices of multicul-turalism in education are related to the new imperatives of globalization, as perceived by neoliberal politicians and educators. Those pushing a neoliberal agenda stress competitiveness for the global knowledge economy alongside the necessity for greater market choice and account-ability. These contemporary strategies reflect a new, transnational capitalist logic, but one that is frequently promoted by state actors. In order to understand how and why this type of shift occurs it is helpful to review some of the Marxist scholarship on the nexus between schooling, economy, and the state.

Political Economy, State Formation, and Systems of Education

Studies of the articulation of education and the economy relate primarily to examining how systems of public education are and were developed largely for the purpose of sustaining capitalist systems of accumulation. In essence, this work probes the classic question of the relationship between production and social reproduction, using Marxist categories to define and articulate the ways in which the institution of national systems of public education are deeply intertwined with the formation and maintenance of certain kinds of labor under capitalism.

Early work sought to make a direct link between industrialization and the establishment of national systems of education. The broad contention was that as new factories opened up in the nineteenth century, a new workforce was needed, and hence public schooling was initiated so that workers could be trained for this type of labor.[1] Although this direct and obvious link was appealing as an argument, later empirical work indicated that what was actually taught in the early classrooms could not be linked directly with the kinds of skills that were becoming increasingly desirable in the industrial workforce.

A second wave of thought regarding the articulation between education and the economy emphasized the reproduction of the social conditions of capitalist labor rather than the actual production of capitalist laborers. In this literature, schooling was depicted as a key controlling mechanism that could ameliorate some of the social ills associated with the rise of industrial capitalism. As a tool of social management it had the capacity to legitimate inequality, defuse explosive class relations associated with the productive process, and deliver the "appropriate" societal norms and expectations to society's future workers. In other words, as an institution intimately involved in the reproduction of consciousness, education was a key mechanism used by dominant elites to achieve a certain type of subordinate consciousness, which aided in the maintenance of an unequal system of class relations. Bowles and Gintis developed this argument to the fullest degree in their book *Schooling in Capitalist America*.[2]

Even though they agreed with the connection that was made between education and the production of an unequal class system, however, a number of scholars disliked the structuralist tone of this argument. Students and their families seemed too easily "duped" by the system, buying into the dominant ideas of the ruling elite as spread via the school system. Ensuing studies tried to find a balance between the constraining forces of the economy and the agency of individuals and groups in asserting their own sociocultural positions. Thus in *Learning to Labor*, Paul Willis explored students' multiple axes of identity, including masculinity and class culture, which led many of the boys in his study to actively reject school—despite being well aware of the consequences of their choices.[3]

Following this, some scholars started to emphasize the ways in which education was also tied to state formation. Andy Green argued that modern education systems in Europe and North America were an important means for furthering state development with respect to its mercantilist aims and its training programs for bureaucratic positions and state manufacturing projects.[4] National education systems were an integral tool in creating political loyalty, operating to develop, manage, and sustain the types of myths and narratives of the nation crucial to its initial and ongoing unification. In this view, state schooling was not just about the creation of a literate population or a trained workforce, but was implicated more generally in the creation of a particular kind of state subject—one schooled in the norms and proper codes of behavior related to national citizenship.

These twin processes of social reproduction and state formation remain integral to how education strategies are formulated and implemented today, but current transformations in the state's relationship to the global economy have altered how they operate. In the context of deindustrialization, post-Fordism, and new strategies of capital accumulation, the connections between schooling and the economy now revolve around different skill sets and attitudes towards work and nation. These reflect the imperatives of rapidly changing technologies, the rise of just-in-time production and global commodity chains, and new spatial divisions of labor. In this context, national ideologies formerly linked with postwar state formation—such as multiculturalism—have shifted in response to the spatial, digital, cultural, and economic transformations associated with neoliberal globalization, more flexible strategies of capital accumulation, and the rise of the knowledge economy. In the following sections I look at some specific shifts in the pronouncements and policies of multicultural education in three different societies.

Multiculturalism in Education

Ideologically, multiculturalism functioned for many years as a national narrative of coherence and unification in countries with large immigrant, aboriginal, and minority populations. For Canada in particular, multiculturalism—or cultural pluralism as it was initially termed—was an official doctrine that in the early years allowed an uneasy truce to be formed between the original two colonizing powers, the British and the French. In later decades it represented an effort to inculcate immigrants and First Nations people into a national mosaic, where difference was professed to be both welcome and advantageous. For Canada, and to a lesser degree for the United States and United Kingdom, the concept of multicultural citizenship and the practices of multicultural education following World War II served as an example of the tolerant and munificent liberal state, willing to open its doors to immigrants, and to accept and protect individual and cultural differences within the national community.

Multicultural education in liberal, anglophone societies such as these was largely concerned with the creation of a national citizen who could learn from, or at the very least be tolerant of, individual, cultural, and ethnic differences in diverse school populations. But these differences were always framed within certain national parameters and managed by the institutions of the state. Progressives and conservatives in the three countries found common ground in the utilization of multiculturalism as a containing metaphor for difference, although with different opinions as to the relative merits of state-sanctioned multicultural practices in education and other institutions through time.

The timing of this positive orientation of the state to multiculturalism is important to consider. The narrative of multiculturalism in the service of national unity operated as a conceptual philosophy primarily during the postwar, Fordist regime. During this period the economies of Canada, the United Kingdom, and the United States grew rapidly, but they were also relatively protected from outside competition. Unlike the ensuing period of neoliberal globalization, there was greater (although never complete) consensus on the relative benefits of state intervention in the economy, and the relationship between capital and labor was more highly regulated. At the same time, immigration from non-Western countries increased rapidly during these years.

In this time period, multiculturalism in education operated effectively as an instrument of state management at a number of levels. This included serving as a national narrative of coherence in the face of immigrant difference, as a way the state could exhibit the management and control of difference, and in the attempt to constitute national citizens willing to work harmoniously with immigrants and others perceived as either culturally or racially different from a white citizenship norm. Further, as a national narrative of harmony, multiculturalism presented an image of tolerance and calm in the context of the increasing visibility of institutional racism and the rise of antiracist social movements and forms of civil disobedience in the postwar period. In some contexts it functioned to dilute or defer stronger expressions of group-based cultural identity— such as by the Québécois in Canada; in others it was part of a broader attempt to neutralize or depoliticize more radical activist efforts against state-based forms of racism.[5]

In a number of diverse contexts the rhetoric of multiculturalism also provided a corporate cover for conducting business as usual. In some cases this involved embracing tolerance for superficial expressions of cultural difference (such as in food or dress) while deeper processes of racism and economic inequity were left unaddressed. In others the narrative of multiculturalism was wielded more aggressively to promote capitalist interests. For example, during the 1980s in British Columbia, a number of real estate institutes, investors, and state actors affiliated with the red-hot Vancouver property market tried to counteract slow-growth movements by claiming that they were racist efforts to keep out Chinese property buyers. These actors used the rhetoric of multicultural tolerance in an effort to both attract international Hong Kong capitalists to invest further in the city, while simultaneously attacking all who opposed unfettered market development as anti-Chinese. The latter position was also depicted as anti-Canadian, since multiculturalism was projected as a key narrative underpinning national identity.[6]

In all of these ways, multiculturalism served as a strategic partner in the growth and expansion of the capitalist regime of accumulation during the Fordist period. Despite its claims of ongoing tolerance and universal inclusion, it was a philosophy that was, in many ways, quite specific to its time and place. Moreover, although multicultural practices often had important positive effects in individual schools, multiculturalism itself functioned largely as a liberal panacea to the wider problems associated with capitalist and racist societies, most of which were left underfunded or unaddressed.

With the end of Fordism, and the rise of contemporary transnational lives and neoliberal pressures, the state promotion of multiculturalism began to decline. While the commitment of many individual teachers and local schools to multicultural education has continued, neoliberal politicians at the state level began to perceive the rhetoric of multiculturalism as either irrelevant or negative. They pushed for stronger commitments to national assimilation, more strategic skills to be taught in school, and for students to become more business oriented, entrepreneurial, and competitive. This shift began towards the end of the twentieth century and has continued in various forms through the present. To illustrate some of these general trends empirically, I provide three brief case studies from Canada, England, and the United States.

Case Study: Canada

Canada's system of public education was developed primarily in the period between 1840 and 1870, and was part of a deliberate strategy by political liberals to forge a new political nationality.[7] Although there was little formal opposition to the expansion of a national system of education, differences in language and religion between the two colonizing powers led to major divisions in the form and content of educational curricula and pedagogic philosophies. The deep divisions played out in the formation of distinct educational regimes between the provinces, as well as in a general geographic decentralization of the educational system.

The British North America Act of 1867 (now the Constitution Act) united the colonies in a federal system under the British Crown, and gave the provincial legislatures exclusive jurisdiction to make education-related laws. This early provincial independence increased the already broad differentiation among the provinces in terms of language of instruction, secularism, and denominationalism, as well as in the more general attitude toward the political philosophy of liberalism itself. Despite these ongoing differences, however, a fairly broad consensus developed over time regarding the benefits of liberalism and the schooling of children in political liberties and civic obligations.[8]

Although the system was decentralized and there were variations among the provinces, the galvanizing force behind most educational policies and practices was the broad understanding that public schools were crucial institutions in shaping the incipient national character. As Canadian identity consolidated in the nineteenth century, the national education system was put to work to manipulate, mold, and otherwise inculcate, "the state of the public mind."[9] Egerton Ryerson, the linchpin of educational reform in Ontario (and widely influential throughout Canada) in the mid-nineteenth century, firmly believed in the power of education to create model Canadian citizens and patriots who could be depended on to uphold the status quo and support the state in times of crisis.[10]

The general tone of educational policy from its development in the nineteenth century through the middle of the twentieth reflected a political liberalism that was premised on the overriding belief that individual opportunity and equal access to education, coupled with a strongly hierarchical and divided system of occupational classes, would benefit both the socioeconomic order and state formation. Industrial expansion, state formation, and national-character development could all be accommodated within the broad tenets of liberalism, despite provincial variations based on differing languages and religious denominations.

Beginning in the postwar period and gaining ground in the late 1950s and 1960s, however, a different strand of liberalism began to hold sway among a number of educational authorities. This new framework, what Manzer termed "ethical liberalism," drew intellectual sustenance from the ideas of philosophers such as John Dewey. Dewey had long argued for a greater focus on the development of each individual to his or her fullest personal potential through educational programs geared to the "real world" situations of plural, diverse, and communicative democracy. Ethical liberalism was a humanistic philosophy emphasizing the specific differences and needs of each individual child, and the necessity of tailoring the system of schooling to fulfill those needs. Further, it was broadly inclusive, providing special opportunities for talented or challenged children, but also bringing students considered "different" back into a mainstream learning environment.

In this educational framework, a single type of education could never accommodate all of the different variations of student needs and learning styles. Thus it behooved the authorities to provide a highly differentiated, flexible, and forgiving system, one wherein each person could reach personal fulfillment in whatever path he or she might choose. One of the primary features of this mode of learning was the fundamental acknowledgement of the wide scope of difference within human society, and of the necessity to embrace this difference through daily interaction in schools, as well as in society at large.

Borrowing from the English liberal tradition of John Stuart Mill and the American tradition of Dewey, the framework of ethical liberalism quickly became an established force in Canadian educational circles, achieving some degree of hegemony in the decades of the 1960s and 1970s. As with Dewey's pronouncements on democratic citizenship in the United States, ethical liberalism in Canada quickly became bound up with a strongly nationalist agenda. During the 1960s, Canada experienced rapidly increasing immigration from non-European regions of the world, and was also rocked by violent expressions of dissent from Quebec, culminating in the Quiet Revolution. At the same time, First Nations groups began to organize and make claims for cultural rights, land, and economic reparations for hundreds of years of oppression at the hands of the dominant colonial powers. The promotion of ethical liberalism was quickly wrapped in the mantle of ethnic tolerance and utilized as part of a newly stylish cultural pluralism (multiculturalism) that was intended to placate immigrants, the French, and "the natives," all in one fell swoop.

The tolerant Canadian state, held together by narratives of unity with and through difference, was a key touchstone of multiculturalism in education. During this period students were taught that the Canadian cultural mosaic was a defining feature of Canadianness, and that multiculturalism was the superior method for the integration of immigrants. The concept of multiculturalism contained, as a foundational core, the belief that working with and through cultural difference was a key to participatory democracy, and that local communities must maintain their autonomy and distinctive traditions in order for this democracy to work. A key geographical component of ethical liberalism thus took shape in the advocacy of a continued decentralization of educational policy and practice. It was believed that decentralization would allow for more egalitarian decision-making and a greater inclusion of difference, and thus extend the multicultural and democratic mantle nationwide.

At the same time as this educational framework was extended, the Fordist period of capital accumulation took shape. The state increasingly regulated business and extended social services to a wider group of citizens. The Canadian welfare state grew rapidly, expanding in areas such as national health care, public housing, unemployment insurance, care of the indigent, children, and the elderly, and a number of other venues.

Although multiculturalism in education was widely accepted and implemented through most of the Canadian system in the 1960s and 1970s, it was always opposed by rival theories which foregrounded greater structure, standards, and traditional methods of teaching. The proponents of greater standardization in education began a concerted attack on ethical liberalism in the late 1970s, and defeated some of the innovations of the prior two decades. By the late 1980s and early 1990s, both policy and practice in education reflected a shifting (though still highly contested) mood of politicians and administrators toward a new framework of educational "excellence," perceived to be more appropriate for facing the pressures and challenges of the new global economy. These shifts accompanied a large-scale attack on the rhetoric and practices of welfarism in Canada, and the rapid entrenchment of neoliberal policy throughout the 1990s.[11]

In the late 1980s, two major reports on public education were published, both of which expressed criticism of the current system.[12] The two reports were cited extensively by business interests and federal agencies in the following years as "proof" that the national experiment in multiculturalism was a failure, that the educational quality of state-funded schools was declining, and that Canadian students were rapidly falling behind their peers in crucial areas such as math and science. In one of the reports, the link between investing in a new kind of education and creating a new kind of work force was blunt and categorical. George Radwanski, a Canadian journalist hired by the Ontario premier to investigate the province's drop-out rate, wrote in the report: "Education has long been recognized as an important contributor to economic growth, of course—but now it has become *the* paramount ingredient for competitive success in the world economy." He went on to conclude that multiculturalism and learning about racism was unnecessary "stuff" littering the curriculum. According to Radwanski it was no longer a relevant educational framework, given the new kinds of technological needs and employment possibilities of the global economy.[13]

Struggles over educational priorities and philosophies continued throughout the 1990s, with provinces often establishing a particular kind of program based on one philosophy or another, only to reverse it a few years later based either on a change of government or a change of heart. In 1991, the Progressive Conservative government under its prime minister Brian Mulroney attempted to direct educational administrators away from the more "unstructured" learning environments of multicultural classrooms and towards a more skills-based curriculum, especially in the fields of science and technology.[14] Although this initial move was not particularly successful, it was accompanied by a constant rhetoric that state schools were failing, which had the desired effect of producing anxiety among parents, and hence the ongoing possibility of a major reorganization of the system, which occurred over the next two decades.

Throughout the 1990s and 2000s, antagonists of multiculturalism formed institutions that countered multicultural ideology with a constant refrain of excellence, accountability, global competitiveness, and choice, which they juxtaposed negatively with the current educational system. In the classroom itself, opponents of multicultural education demanded an externally established curriculum, frequent testing, mandated letter grades, quantitative accountability standards, and a "back to basics" method of teaching. These demands were frequently backed by both provincial and federal legislation mandating more standardized testing across all grades, as well as greater accountability measures for students' academic performance and for systems of state school financing.

Alongside these philosophical and practical changes there was a strong shift in the geography of control over schools themselves. Beginning in the 1990s, nearly every province in the country reduced the number of school boards that were active in educational decision-making. In Ontario, this move was accompanied by legislation in 1998 that, through the imposition of educational property taxes, shifted school board control over financing to provincial control. Overall, these changes reflected a sharp transition from Canada's earlier decentralized system of educational governance, one that further enabled neoliberal directives from above to be diffused downward through local systems.

Over the past decade and a half many of these neoliberal reforms have continued, with recent studies indicating both increased market-oriented reforms and declining political interest in the promotion or implementation of multicultural policies. Alongside federal decreases in funding for education there has been an increase in school choice and other forms of incipient educational privatization. This has been accompanied by greater economic and racial segregation, as middle-class white parents tend to choose and help fund specialty arts programs, advanced curricular and extracurricular activities, and schools that prepare students for college and economic success, while, because of residential constraints and community support systems, "low-income, racially marginalized families tend to choose schools in their neighborhoods."[15]

This brief study of multicultural education in Canada was intended to highlight the association between a liberal narrative of cultural tolerance and a particular capitalist regime of accumulation, as well as the moment of transition to a different era. As a national narrative of unity in diversity, multiculturalism served as an important strategy of state formation and tool of governance at a specific moment in time, one that was adopted and advocated with enthusiasm and sincerity by a number of educators and schools. With the advent and growth of neoliberalism in the late twentieth century, however, there was a noticeable shift in the pronouncements and policies of state actors and institutions at the higher levels of government. While always contested and often ignored at the level of local schools, this general shift in tone reflected these broader, global socioeconomic transformations.

I next explore some of the similarities between Canada's case and what happened in England over the same time period. There are of course numerous differences between these societies not enumerated in depth here. My aim is to indicate some of the general trends that can be identified so as to make a larger argument about the articulation of economy, society, and schooling and its geographical underpinnings.

Case Study: England

A national system of state-funded education did not develop in England until late in the nineteenth century. Even at this relatively late date, the implementation of the system was weak, with little financing set aside for education, and with no unified central authority to monitor its progress or development. As a result, national education developed slowly and sporadically throughout the country and remained highly stratified between state and private systems. There was little uniformity of curricula, methods, or teacher training between different schools, no integrated policy of admissions, fees, or examination systems, and no coherent plan for the linkages between elementary, secondary, and higher education. Up until quite recently there was no educational constitution, a minimal parliamentary role in education, and little sense of a unified or integrated national system.[16]

These divergent policies and practices were reflected most conspicuously in the deep and ongoing divide between state and private schools. In a manner similar to Canada, the national system of education served to reproduce and legitimate dominant class relations.[17] But unlike in Canada, state-funded education was not called upon to assist in state formation through the constitution of properly disciplined national subjects oriented towards a newly unified national identity. It was not until World War II and the early postwar years that the institution of education began to play a more active role in this regard.

This was a period of educational transformation in which spending on education increased dramatically, and more general policies of economic and social reform were put in place to raise the living standards of working-class people. These included a major program of public housing, redistributive taxation policies, and the establishment of the National Health Service.[18] More generally, this early period reflected the Fordist economic policies of state interventionism, where the state's role in regulation, planning, and equitable redistribution was considered to be an efficient system of capital accumulation.

Following the British Nationality Act of 1948, in which Commonwealth citizens were admitted as British subjects, immigration from non-European regions, particularly from the West Indies and then South Asia, increased dramatically. Initially, the education system remained strongly monocultural in orientation, stressing the English language and cultural mores, and advocating complete assimilation to "Britishness." Within a decade, however, assimilationist policies began to be contested, and the philosophy of multiculturalism in education assumed a more dominant role. In articles and government reports of this period, there was an emerging narrative on the importance of allowing cultural difference to be expressed in schools (for example, trousers or hijab for Muslim girls, and turbans for Sikh boys).[19]

Alongside these somewhat tentative expressions of tolerance for cultural difference was a growing exploration of new ways of thinking about individual learning differences. Manifested most concretely in the influential Plowden Report of 1967, these ideas challenged the established practices of streaming (wherein children at very young ages are channeled into different educational "tracks" based on examinations), and introduced more progressive notions of child-centered pedagogy, activity-based learning, and the importance of acknowledging social and economic factors outside of the classroom that impacted children's learning.

The public recognition and acceptance of different immigrant cultures was important, but it was often socially and economically disconnected from the real life experiences of most immigrants, in which racism and economic inequity were rife. The superficial flavor of welcome and tolerance was soon ridiculed as a multiculturalism of the three Ss: saris, samosas, and steel bands.[20] A stronger movement for antiracist education developed in the 1970s, with impetus from migrant communities as well as progressive educators on the Left. However, both movements had limitations and attracted different constituencies,[21] and they remained at odds through the 1980s—a fracturing that made it even more difficult to counter the conservative backlash against all progressive educational reforms that gained in strength with the election of Margaret Thatcher as Prime Minister in 1979.

The significance of race in the country's institutions and politics was obvious to those experiencing rampant racism in housing, employment, and education, but it was given national prominence by the infamous "Rivers of Blood" speech by Enoch Powell in 1968.[22] According to the British educational historian Ken Jones, it is "impossible to understand the politics of education in the 1970s—and later—without appreciating the ways in which they were shaped by cultural meanings and conflicts in which questions of 'race' and 'nation' played a central part."[23] The more inclusive, child-centered, activity-based, multiculturalist, and antiracist educational reforms of the 1960s and 1970s were bound up and rejected by conservatives in a combined narrative of threat and danger, a narrative given voice and amplified by Powell's speech.

The "threat" of multiculturalism and antiracist policies in education thus became part of a broader backlash pursued by conservatives in the 1980s that sought to roll back all of the postwar changes of the Fordist era.[24] Despite committee findings such as the Rampton Report of 1981, which described the devastating impact of racism on black school-children, the Conservative government under Thatcher made little effort to continue the educational reforms of the earlier two decades. Indeed, there was active opposition to most of the earlier reforms, manifested most clearly in some of the legislation of the succeeding decade. In 1988, for example, the government rolled out its Education Reform Act (ERA), which, although continuing to express a bland narrative of cultural tolerance, effectively undid the Rampton Report's strong antiracist language and recommendations for reform.

The ERA introduced three major changes to the educational system, all of which rapidly moved it in a neoliberal direction. The first was a shift to a school-based system of financial management, away from the control of the generally more progressive Local Education Authorities (LEAs). The second was a provision for schools to "opt out" of LEA control and become "grant maintained" schools, receiving funding directly from central government. The third change was the development of a national curriculum. Although packaged as a move towards greater geographical decentralization, in effect these three reforms massively increased central control over both the structure and organization of local authorities, and over individual schools themselves. The introduction of a national curriculum effectively gutted the possibility for further multi-cultural educational initiatives in education, since all schools were now forced to adopt the same curriculum, which was based on the concept that all children had the same opportunities, rights, and access. In other words, there was no recognition of the challenges of cultural, economic, or individual differences that might impact children's learning.

The standardization and homogenization of the curriculum facilitated the possibility for more standardized tests, which soon followed. As with the neoliberal shifts in education in Canada during the same period, the language in which these reforms were promoted revolved around three key words: choice, excellence, and accountability. They were also accompanied by the same insistent drumbeat of state school decline and the necessity to reform them in order to meet the challenges of the new global economy.

The transition to school-based financial management was part of a broader neoliberal strategy at the start of the third term of Thatcher's Conservative Party government (re-elected in 1987), which emphasized the restructuring of local authority service provision. The general approach was to encourage the private sector through contracting out delivery services. This form of privatization was extended to a wide range of services in addition to education, and it represented a strong shift to a governmental system of contract management. In addition to weakening LEAs, this form of private contracting controlled by central government facilitated the hiring of teachers from outside commonwealth countries. This group could be paid less than those with British citizenship, and were brought in to weaken the power of the teachers' unions.

Thus, although contested and with uneven effects across the country, there was a general shift in the philosophy of state education in England beginning most dramatically in the late 1980s. It was one that directed education away from the reformist possibilities of child-centered learning and knowledge about diverse groups, as well as of considering the "whole" child—that is, taking into consideration the effects of structural processes such as classism, sexism, and racism outside of the classroom. Thus both multicultural and antiracist aims and practices of recognizing difference and tackling racism were rapidly squelched with the rise of the Thatcher government.

A pro-business, market friendly set of policies was integral to Thatcher's neoliberal restructuring of the economy. These were manifested in educational policy with the mantra of parental choice. At the same time, much of Thatcher's support derived from her cultural conservatism, reflected in ideologies of English traditional values and nostalgia for a purer, more authentic national community. As Stuart Hall and Paul Gilroy have pointed out, this latter narrative rested on the implicit articulation of cultural tradition and whiteness, such that black immigrants were always characterized as existing outside of the beloved cultural practices and traditions of British nationalism.[25]

Thatcher's conservative educational policies attempted to encapsulate both the neoliberal orientation to free markets, global competition, flexible lives, and parental choice, *and* neoconservative ideas of national cultural restoration—embodying everything from traditional learning styles to established hierarchies of schooling and culture. These two positions were often antithetical, however, and the Conservative Party was defeated in the general election of 1997. The ensuing New Labour government of Tony Blair adopted the so-called "third way," a policy position attempting to steer a middle road between a neoliberal reliance on (global) markets and government management of select national institutions and programs—such as education. Often this management involved partnerships between the public and private sectors.

New Labour's efforts in this spirit entailed creating the educational context in which national subjects could be effectively trained to succeed in a globalized economy. For Blair, this meant education for the knowledge economy. He believed government should prepare its workers with the skills necessary to implement the new technologies of a changing world, one of rapid transformation and intense global competition. David Blunkett, Tony Blair's first minister of education, made it clear that economic needs and goals would drive government policy. And Peter Mandelson, secretary of trade and industry, said in a speech, "Knowledge and its profitable exploitation by business is the key to competitiveness."[26]

Although rhetorically sympathetic to questions of social inclusion, the strong normative drive of preparation for educational success and global competitiveness created the conditions in which cultural difference, racism, and other problems encountered both inside and outside the classroom were effectively elided. These types of broader concerns were devolved to parents, family, and the community. When Blunkett said, for example, "we need parents who are prepared to take responsibility for supporting their children's education," it was an implicit critique of the earlier multiculturalists and other reformers who sought to make cultural and class differences, racism, and similar issues relevant to educational policy.[27] For Blunkett, it was the responsibility of students and their families to choose schools wisely, adapt, and succeed.

Thus, similar in many ways to the preceding regime, but without the more obviously regressive cultural baggage, New Labour retained the educational goals of parental responsibility, strategic learning, and global market success. And similar to Canada during the same time period, it was the advent of neoliberalism that marked the shift from the multicultural and antiracist programs of the postwar period to this type of strategic cosmopolitanism. While the United Kingdom never implemented multicultural education programs to the same extent as Canada, the period from the mid-1960s through the early 1980s witnessed a number of reforms that were either ended or redirected in more economically strategic ways by both the Conservatives and New Labour. I next turn to the United States, which provides a third and final example of this general trend.

Case Study: The United States

Unlike the United Kingdom, there was widespread early support for establishing systems of publicly funded education in the United States. The major struggle in the US context revolved more around the degree of local versus federal control. By and large, early schools developed locally, often out of previously established private or religious schools, and the national system remained highly decentralized for decades. Over time, autonomous, district schools became absorbed into a centralized system of town schools, but the highest level of control remained at the state level, with little or no federal intervention through the mid-twentieth century.[28]

In the mid-nineteenth century, public education was linked with national narratives of personal freedom, social mobility, and the opportunity for individuals to become active laborers within a dynamic capitalist system. Children were schooled in the ultimate freedom of the individual, but also in the appropriate mode of operating as upright and moral citizens within the national community. In this vein, there was a concentrated drive toward assimilating immigrants and minority cultures into a common Anglo-Protestant culture. This involved separation from what were seen to be inferior cultural habits and re-education into the superior norms and values of a dominant white culture.[29] The link between the indoctrination of a proper national citizen in this manner, and the inculcation of work habits and beliefs beneficial to the development of capitalism, was strongly apparent throughout this early period.[30]

Although there were many reformist impulses through the twentieth century, it was not until the 1960s that the philosophy of pluralist democracy, or multiculturalism, began to attain some real purchase within the public education system. A number of federal education laws were passed in the late 1950s and 1960s that guaranteed more accordance with the nation's liberal values and narrative of equal access and opportunity. These included the National Defense Education Act of 1958 and the Elementary and Secondary Education Act of 1965, both of which expanded educational opportunity for the poor and increased federal financing in selected areas. Additionally, after decades of strategizing by lawyers from the NAACP (National Association for the Advancement of Colored People), a number of local lawsuits challenging segregation were combined in the Supreme Court case of *Brown v. Board of Education of Topeka* in 1954.[31] Victory in this major case showed a stronger national commitment to challenging segregation and racial disparities in educational equity and access, although the majority of local schools remained segregated for decades.

Similar to Canada and the United Kingdom, postwar struggles for greater resources and equitable opportunities led to an expansion of the state role in a number of other social and economic institutions as well. State intervention in the United States was characterized by increased planning, more regulation of the wage relation and labor market policies, and higher social benefits. While Fordism never attained the same level of development in the United States as it did in numerous other postwar liberal regimes (for example, a national health care service was not created during this time), it was nevertheless the dominant mode of growth until the fiscal crisis and stagflation of the mid 1970s.

The case of *Brown v. Board of Education* opened the possibilities for nationwide integration and the introduction of more multicultural practices into schools. In the US context these practices included new instruction materials and ways of teaching that were intended to widen students' knowledge of diverse cultural traditions and the historical contributions of non-white groups.[32] They were also aimed at promoting principles of inclusion and democratic participation, as well as acceptance of children's individual learning styles and social and emotional differences. In the latter case, reformers also drew on the works of John Dewey, who wrote, "A democracy is more than a form of government; it is primarily a mode of associated living, of conjoint communicated experience."[33] For these educators it was the combination of multiculturalism and multiracialism that was integral to the formation and maintenance of a democratic society.[34]

Although generally promoted as a widely inclusive and universal vision, the utilization of Dewey's ideas was very clearly set within the American postwar national context. Tackling the legacies of Jim Crow apartheid in schools and society more generally was critical for establishing the United States as a modern, unified, and progressive nation. Evidence of racial disenfranchisement at home—so clearly identified in Gunnar Myrdal's widely disseminated 1944 book, *An American Dilemma: The Negro Problem and Modern Democracy*—was a hindrance to the exportation of liberalism and capitalism abroad, and to the imperial ambitions of the United States during this time period.[35] The promotion from above of desegregation, cultural pluralism, and improved race relations was thus part of a wider strategy of national unification and state propaganda intended to demonstrate both domestically and internationally that the so-called "Negro problem" was under control.

At the scale of schools and social movements from below, however, efforts to promote racial integration and introduce multicultural education into the classroom were a constant struggle. The Civil Rights Act of 1964 and the Bilingual Education Act of 1968 were integral in furthering these two goals, and the period between 1968 and 1980 saw the greatest successes in school desegregation. At the same time, multicultural education became both more inclusive, vis-à-vis educational equity for people with disabilities, LGBT students, and low-income groups, and more mainstream in teaching materials and methods.[36]

While always contested, these incipient reforms came under increasing attack following the election of the Republican Party candidate Ronald Reagan as president in 1980. The impact of his administration's strongly neoliberal agenda began to be felt in education almost immediately. For example, the National Commission on Excellence in Education delivered a scathing indictment of the public education system in a report entitled "A Nation at Risk: The Imperative for Educational Reform" in 1983.[37] This official report was the first of a series of government proclamations attacking the public education system, part of a concerted campaign to depict schools as failing and to weaken support and faith in the system. It was followed with an anxiety-producing narrative of a national lack of competitiveness in comparison with other nations, caused primarily by poor educational preparation. Picking up on this theme, some commentators even suggested that American schools were to blame for the country's declining predominance in the international marketplace. The ongoing refrain of the report and those that followed was the massive failure of the educational system to prepare students for employment in the changing world economy. For example, in the report of the Economic Growth Task Force in the same year, it was stated that federally funded schools "are not doing an adequate job of education for today's requirements" in the workplace, much less tomorrow's."[38]

These reports were accompanied by numerous critiques of the previous era of educational reforms by conservative thinkers and media pundits. In addition to the constant refrain of public school failure, the need for higher standards, and the necessity for more attention to STEM (science, technology, engineering and math) subjects, conservative educators and administrators began to lead a concerted attack on the philosophy of multiculturalism itself. Assistant Secretary of Education Chester Finn's statement in 1982 is representative of this discourse:

> The sad fact is that for close to two decades now we have neglected educational quality in the name of equality. Trying to insure that every child would have access to as much education as every other child, we have failed to attend to the content of that education. Seeking to mediate conflict and forestall controversy over the substance of education, we begin to find ourselves with very little substance needed. Striving to avoid invidious comparisons among youngsters we have stopped gauging individual progress by testing ... Hesitant to pass judgement on lifestyles, cultures and forms of behavior we have invited relativism into the curriculum and pedagogy.[39]

In their book *Education under Siege*, Aronowitz and Giroux noted how Finn's statement suggested that practices of equality and social inclusion led to the overall weakening of academic excellence.[40] After this time the mantra of excellence began to pervade educational discourse from pre-kindergarten classes through the university. And throughout the 1990s various kinds of testing and accountability measures were introduced in every state and at every grade level. Much of the new testing culture was framed, yet again, as necessary to prepare children for the changing needs of a highly competitive global economy.

The twin refrain of excellence and global competition was encapsulated in the Education Reform Act, known as No Child Left Behind. This 2001 legislation provided the most sweeping federal-based reform in the United States since the 1950s. In his speech outlining the new act, President George W. Bush invoked the now familiar refrain of public schools as failing—especially with respect to preparation for a changing world. He said:

> The quality of our public schools directly affects us all as parents, as students, and as citizens. Yet too many children in America are segregated by low expectations, illiteracy, and self-doubt. In a constantly changing world that demands increasingly complex skills from its work force, children are being left behind.[41]

Tellingly, the word segregation in this speech no longer referred to racial and class separation caused by racism and poverty, but rather to the cultural values projected as holding children back. In this neoliberal vision of education, educating a child to be a good citizen and successful worker was no longer synonymous with unity in diversity but rather with attainment of the "complex skills" necessary for individual success in a "constantly changing world." As I examine further in Chapter 6, many of these same preoccupations with entrepreneurial competitiveness and success continued under President Barack Obama's educational initiatives, but with new partners and promises.

Multiculturalism Today

Historians of education have documented how the rise and development of national education systems in Western industrial societies was related to both economic development and state formation, particularly with respect to the advancement of social cohesion and national identity. In the postwar period multiculturalism was an important ideology and set of practices in this regard, in the context of strong state intervention in economic regulation, immigration from non-Western societies, and increasing demands for economic opportunity, cultural inclusion, and racial equity. While unevenly implemented and challenged by forces on both the political right and left, multiculturalism was widely promoted for a time by both state politicians and educators as a critical strategy to engage and unify increasingly diverse groups within the nation-state.

Various forms of multicultural education are still practiced in many schools today, and educators continue to debate its radical pedigree. Is multiculturalism primarily a liberal sop—a superficial ideology that enables capitalism and racism to proceed as normal? Does it depoliticize broader claims for equity and social justice under the banner of tolerance and just getting along? Or does multicultural education provide vital ideas and methods for teachers to promote inclusion, respect, and knowledge about different ways of being, doing, and knowing?

These questions cannot be answered adequately in the abstract as the answers depend on the historical and geographical context in which individual educators and students teach and learn from each other. However, independent of these important debates and the continuing hard work of teachers on the ground, the three case studies introduced here indicate the broad forces now arrayed against this philosophy. The world of high-stakes testing and preparation for the global economy is the new coin of the realm, and questions of diversity and equity have receded into the background. These changes reflect the spatial and economic shifts of a new transnational capitalist logic, one that also impacts the world of adult learning, as I examine further in the next chapter.

4

Geographies of Lifelong Learning and the Knowledge Economy

Lifelong learning is traditionally defined as learning that continues throughout one's life and that encompasses both traditional schooling and informal venues and practices. It is a form of learning most frequently undertaken by adults to improve their skills and knowledge so as to gain better employment opportunities. In this view, lifelong learning is a wonderful opportunity, one voluntarily engaged in and frequently enjoyed, leading to personal fulfillment as well as greater professional development and the chance to improve one's life chances.

Lifelong learning can indeed be these things for individual actors, but as a governing concept and set of institutional practices it has broader, frequently negative repercussions for workers and for society as a whole. As discussed in the preceding chapters, the perceived skills necessary for contemporary employment success have shifted over the last few decades. These changes indicate the growth of new global divisions of labor, neoliberal rationalities of governance, and a related demand for the constant retraining, redevelopment, and redeployment of human capital worldwide. In this chapter I am interested in how the concept of lifelong learning was deployed by state actors at different scales of governance, including the supranational European Union (EU), to shift responsibility for retraining to the individual. I show further how the policies and institutions formed on the basis of this concept have worked to secure a capitalist process of exploitation that benefits a global elite far more than individual workers.

Lifelong learning plays a role in the production of space, not just as an abstract governing principle but also as a diverse set of practices and institutions that has developed and transformed over time and scale to address the crises of global capitalism. The concept of lifelong learning was first promoted in the early 1970s by intergovernmental organizations such as the United Nations Educational, Scientific and Cultural Organization (UNESCO) and the Organization for Economic

Cooperation and Development (OECD). Similar in some ways to the formulations of multicultural education during the same time period, many of these organizations introduced ideals of democratic learning and personal development. These liberal ideals of individual freedom and growth were, at the same time, always linked with assumptions of economic necessity.

With the advance of neoliberal globalization in the 1990s, however, lifelong learning emerged in more narrowly strategic forms in the policy frameworks of the United States, Canada, and the EU. Neoliberal policies during this latter era worked to orchestrate personal development within the increasingly flexible processes of global capitalism, placing both within the rhythm of a personal life that must be fulfilled. Such an orchestration produced certain spaces—captured in notions such as the "learning society" and "creative city"—in which citizens were expected to take responsibility for their own human capital development as flexible entrepreneurs. For the majority of the population, however, this process led primarily to their own deskilling. Moreover, not only did lifelong learning strategies promote the standardization and homogenization of educational skills, and thus the abstraction and interchangeability of labor, but they were also bound up with the production of a so-called learning society that demanded increasing levels of external management. In the following sections I look at some of the ramifications of these processes on workers and systems of education.

Freedom and Necessity in Lifelong Learning

It is no accident that the concept of lifelong learning first gained traction in the early 1970s. As noted earlier, this was a time when a new international division of labor was emerging and manufacturing jobs in core countries began moving offshore in greater numbers. Suddenly, large swaths of the workforce became obsolete, possessing skills that were no longer marketable within their national borders. These were primarily blue-collar jobs in heavy industries such as steel and automobile manufacturing, as well as in mining and other forms of resource extraction.

Traditional forms of education—those that ended somewhere in the individual's youth—seemed outdated against this backdrop, failing to meet the demands of a new global economy.[1] The concept of lifelong learning emerged within policy circles and academia as a potential solution to this problem. The underlying assumption throughout this period was that extending education into adulthood could provide a way of retraining workers in core countries, giving them the skills needed to compete in a rapidly globalizing economy.

Despite this clear economic imperative, however, during the 1970s lifelong learning was generally framed as a basic human right. This orientation was manifested in the Third International Conference on Adult Education, held in Tokyo in 1972, where it was declared that "the right of individuals to education, their right to learn and to go on learning, is to be considered on the same basis as their other fundamental rights."[2] This moment marked a strong reinterpretation of the right to education as originally stated in the UN's 1948 Universal Declaration of Human Rights. It seemed that the newly conceptualized human right was no longer ascribed to a time-bound notion of schooling connected to the possibilities of immediate employment, but rather to a process of learning and human development that continued through a person's lifetime.

Owing to the stronger narrative of freedom and human rights in the documents of this era, some scholars argued that the concept and practices of lifelong learning changed radically from this early period vis-à-vis its more contemporary iterations. In this view, the earlier period of lifelong learning encouraged and enabled autonomous individual choices and personal development, but these opportunities were no longer viable in later years, and lifelong learning became more about necessity and economic survival in a rapidly transforming global economy.[3] This scholarly analysis rested on abstract liberal assumptions about the potential for great individual opportunity and freedom in the Fordist period, which underplayed the importance of ongoing structuring forces in economy and society, including differences of race, gender, and age, as well as class position.

A more nuanced analysis situates lifelong learning as a concept and set of practices always implemented within capitalist regimes of accumulation, yet shifting in various ways in response to historical and geographical context. Further, it encompasses variations in identity and social position that are bound up in these broader social and economic forces. The most important of the changes affecting these types of educational processes today are the contemporary forces of globalization and the rise of flexible regimes of accumulation and new spatial divisions of labor. Thus in looking at both the narrative and practices of lifelong learning it is critical to examine the underpinning connections of lifelong learning to broader capitalist dynamics, including processes of commoditization, whereby learning is turned into a possession that can be bought and sold on the marketplace. But at the same time it is equally important to tease out the variations, divergences, and contradictions that occur as lifelong learning is introduced to different groups and taken up in different times and places.

The merging of both freedom and necessity in early lifelong learning formulations is evident in some of the first policy documents published by UNESCO and the OECD.[4] On the one hand, UNESCO and the OECD differed greatly in their approaches. While UNESCO emphasized lifelong learning as a basic human right, the OECD was more concerned with lifelong learning as an economic fix. These rationales were not incompatible, however. On the contrary, when reading the UNESCO and OECD documents side by side, what becomes evident is that the concept of lifelong learning provided a site for joining, and thereby legitimizing, the flexibilization of labor with certain liberal-humanist conceptions of personal development. While the introduction and implementation of lifelong learning has varied in tone and emphasis over time, this basic articulation remains a core feature.

In the OECD document, lifelong learning was endorsed as a way of generating the occupational flexibility necessary to succeed in an economy with constant technological developments and new labor demands. It was imagined that through lifelong learning programs, the unemployed could not only acquire more marketable skills "but also become a manpower reserve on which the various countries' economies could draw."[5] Lifelong learning was thus seen as a way of producing an educated "reserve army of labor" in a period of economic change. Radical critiques of capitalism have noted how this type of reserve army can benefit capitalist economies because it provides an easily exploitable pool of labor, which tends to drive down the average cost of wages for everyone.[6]

What is interesting about the OECD report is how such large-scale economic imperatives were paired with the language of individual choice. Despite the strong emphasis on economic development, the report's authors indicated that lifelong learning would only be successful when conceived and opted into as a process that also benefited individuals. This trend of conceptually binding and blurring economic growth with personal satisfaction and a sense of individual value is one that has continued through the historical trajectory of lifelong learning. In the following section I examine how these intersections were implemented in national policies, which have similarly tied personal growth to issues of employability and economic development.

The Boom Years: Lifelong Learning in the 1990s

It was not until the late 1990s in the United Kingdom, the United States, and Canada, that lifelong learning reached its peak popularity as educational policy. These years saw a flood of policy documents and reports calling for lifelong learning at both national and supranational scales. In Europe, the concept became a key policy agenda in 1996 after the European Commission (EC) christened that year as the European Year of Lifelong Learning.[7] In the United Kingdom, in particular, lifelong learning was an important component of New Labour's education policy. The government's first major statement on it came out in 1998, in an enthusiastic report entitled "The Learning Age: A Renaissance for a New Britain."[8] Similar eagerness was found in North America, where the US Congress ratified the Lifelong Learning Credit (LLC) in 1997 and the Canadian government rolled out the Lifelong Learning Plan (LLP) in the federal budget for 1998.[9]

Consistent across these policy documents was the view of education as a strategic economic investment. This was typical of the kind of "third way" politics popular in these countries at the time, under the leadership of Tony Blair in the United Kingdom, Bill Clinton in the United States, and Jean Chrétien in Canada. While third-way politics played out differently in each of these countries, there was a similar emphasis on investments in personal development, responsibility, and equal opportunity through market-based solutions rather than via centralized government programs. The most infamous example of this was in the move from welfare to workfare under President Clinton.

The shift in the social safety net from government provision to one of individual responsibility was particularly evident in education. Blair's position was manifested most clearly in "The Learning Age," a government report in which lifelong learning was held up as a tool for developing "the skills, knowledge and understanding that are essential for employability and fulfilment."[10] Notions of personal growth and well-being were repeatedly and insistently connected with economic strategies, inseparable from the essential ability to sell one's labor on the global market. Thus, under the aegis of New Labour's policies on lifelong learning, personal fulfillment and employability came to mean the same thing. Moreover, the necessity to opt in to this neoliberal nexus of human capital development—or suffer the consequences—was quite explicit.

In the United States and Canada during the same time period, lifelong learning policy was also tied to personal growth and individual income set within the framework of the new global economy. Canada's LLP, for instance, was one of several Canadian federal policies on education and training implemented with the explicit intention of developing a high-skilled knowledge economy.[11] It allowed individuals to withdraw money from their registered retirement savings plans to enroll in higher education or training programs for at least three months. The ways in which these loan-based policies were set up urged individuals formerly disconnected or excluded from the global economy to reskill themselves and become responsible entrepreneurial actors in the new era.[12]

Canada's LLP provides an excellent example of neoliberal governance, wherein policies promoted at the state level devolve the responsibility for successful labor market access and employment to the individual. In comparison with the preceding Fordist regime, where the state was involved in and responsible for producing the conditions for full employment, both the risk and the responsibility of employment now fell completely to the individual worker. This worker, moreover, had to understand the optimal conditions for employment, prepare himself or herself for these opportunities—even prospective ones—and pay for the possibility of success out of retirement accounts, thus effectively withdrawing on his/her own future.[13] The individual thus became financially indebted to his or her future self, and encouraged to act and self-manage in ways that ensured that educational investments actually paid off economically. Indeed, the government's explicit goal for this loan was to enable individuals to increase their earning potential, framing education solely as a means of access to future global marketability.

The LLC in the United States worked a bit differently, but maintained a similar third-way politics of individual responsibility. Rather than withdrawing money from a retirement fund, the LLC provided students with a nonrefundable tax credit for postsecondary education expenses. The LLC was part of a larger overhaul of the way that government financed higher education, and included other programs such as the Hope Scholarship Credit (later replaced by the American Opportunity Tax Credit), an expansion of savings plans such as education IRAs (individual retirement accounts), and student loan interest deductions. These changes occurred at both the federal and state level in the United States throughout the 1990s, amidst rising tuition rates, reduced funding for public institutions of higher learning, and an increasingly inadequate supply of direct grants for student aid.[14]

The LLC and Hope Scholarship, the largest of these education initiatives, represented a shift away from needs-based federal programs. Tied to tax liability, these programs offered no direct scholarships to pay for the rising costs of tuition. Lower income families had to resort to other means of paying the upfront costs of college, such as taking out loans. Using the tax system to subsidize higher education thus worked to indirectly shift responsibility from government services onto the individual to pay for his or her own education. At the same time, for those who received tax credits, the savings appeared less as a free welfare handout, and more as a reward for "good behavior"—in the sense of being employed (having a taxable income) and choosing to invest in education or lifelong learning. Indirectly, therefore, the individual was nudged into and made responsible within certain normative value systems—systems that aligned with the social reproduction of capitalist relations.

In practice, this type of individual responsibilization did not play out evenly across social divisions of class, gender, race, and age. In Canada, for example, while the LLP and similar federal education policies claimed to enable equal access, in fact they continued to exclude the most marginalized segments of the population. Individuals could withdraw from their registered retirement savings plans in order to improve their earning potential only if they had already earned enough to contribute to a retirement account in the first place.[15] As such, the LLP served to help those already relatively well off. Similar arguments were made about the LLC in the United States, which was explicitly conceived to aid middle-class Americans. Most low-income students had no tax liability and were therefore not eligible to receive the LLC tax credit.

Although there were other federal programs to assist low-income students such as the Pell Grant in the United States, it is nonetheless significant that federal policy on lifelong learning in both countries offered minimal benefits to those out of work or precariously employed. In some ways, policies such as the LLC and LLP worked to actively produce this precarity, insofar as the solutions offered were limited to the market mechanisms that produced these vulnerabilities in the first place. Through the economization of education and personal development, other potential forms of addressing insecurity—for example, through resource distribution or mutual aid—were ignored or deemed financially imprudent.

From Integration to Responsibilization in the EU

In the preceding section I investigated some of the ways that state policies associated with lifelong learning were introduced in the United States, Canada, and the United Kingdom at the turn of the twenty-first century. Many of these emphases can also be seen in the EU, but there were some interesting differences as well. In some ways similar to the postwar discourse of multiculturalism in England, the earlier iterations of lifelong learning in the EU contained a stronger narrative of social inclusion and the value of cultural diversity with respect to minority integration into European society. But this emphasis began to erode in the context of neoliberal pressures towards strategic learning for the global knowledge economy.

Although neoliberal ideas and actors started to dominate policymaking in the 1990s, they operated in tension with more interventionist programs initiated in the earlier era. Internal divisions and struggles over these programs were particularly evident in the realm of social policy and the politics of European social cohesion. In the sphere of education and training, the EU's primary role was to support its member states and to address what were considered to be common challenges for all nations. These included the ageing of the population, the changing skills needed for the European workforce as a whole, technological transformations, and global competition. With the broad shift towards more *laissez-faire* practices and beliefs, education became a critical site of struggle over the funding priorities and institutional policies associated with these common challenges. Lifelong learning was one of the many mandates caught up in this struggle, as an interest in diversity and social cohesion slowly lost ground to a more economistic logic of governance.

The shift in the EU's educational emphasis was particularly evident in the policy orientation of the 1999 Treaty of Amsterdam, among other treaties of that time period. Programs promoting state intervention, including attempts to encourage cohesive European social communities, began to lose ground to a more economistic emphasis following the treaty's passage. Rather than the social control of labor through the management of difference, EU programs started to focus more on strategies of skills-based training designed to forge all students (both native-born and immigrant) into European citizens via an increasingly cross-border intra-EU labor market.

Lifelong learning was a prominent feature in the so-called "employment chapter" of the Amsterdam Treaty. The employment chapter called on member states to coordinate their employment policy with respect to four common pillars: employability, entrepreneurship, adaptability, and equal opportunities. The type of employment that was envisioned in the treaty was flexible employment, and the laborers who were to provide the workforce were required to be adaptable and entrepreneurial if they expected to obtain and retain jobs. This emphasis on workers' employability rather than workplace conditions represented a significant change in EU policy. According to one labor historian, the policy action areas of the employment chapter "represent[ed] a major shift in social policy" away from universal labor mandates and standards and toward a vision of employment as the key to maintaining the European social model.[16]

In this vision, lifelong learning was explicitly linked with the promotion of a skilled and adaptable labor force for the new, so-called "Europe of knowledge." In EC policy documents of this time period the necessity of constant personal mobilization, or what was then termed "updating," was a frequent refrain in reference to lifelong learning, and was inevitably linked with the employment requirements of a rapidly changing world. Further, successful employment was implicitly associated with successful citizenship. The following quote, from the 1997 EC document, "Towards a Europe of Knowledge," was one of the first discussions of the new strategies for education and training in general, and of lifelong learning in particular, that was envisioned for the EC's policy agenda of 2000–2006:

> Real wealth creation will henceforth be linked to the production and dissemination of knowledge and will depend first and foremost on our efforts in the field of research, education and training and on our capacity to promote innovation. This is why we must fashion a veritable "Europe of knowledge." This process is directly linked to the aim of developing lifelong learning which the Union has set itself and which has been incorporated into the Amsterdam Treaty, expressing the determination of the Union to promote the highest level of knowledge for its people through broad access to education and its permanent updating.[17]

This utilitarian vision of lifelong learning as linked with wealth creation and employability was advanced further by the EU's education commissioner, Viviane Reding, in 2000 and 2001. In the policy agenda of this period there was a clear effort to tie together the commission Directorate of Education and Culture with the Directorate of Employment and Social Affairs. The skills-based, vocational focus of this cooperative strategy was made explicit in related documents and speeches. For example, Anna Diamantopoulou, the commissioner for employment and social affairs, said:

> Skill and competence enhancement in the new economy in Europe requires that the policy emphasis is shifted towards increasing investment in human capital and in raising participation in education and training throughout working life. To keep pace with developments in technology, globalisation, population ageing and new business practices, particular attention should be given to workplace training, an important dimension of our strategy for Lifelong Learning.[18]

In March 2000, the Lisbon meeting of the European Council confirmed lifelong learning as a foundational component of the European social model. Employment was a key agenda item of the Lisbon meeting, as was the objective of shaping a new Europe and becoming "the most competitive and dynamic knowledge-based economy in the world."[19] As a result of the Lisbon recommendations, lifelong learning was allocated significant funding for the period 2000–2006 from the European Social Fund and was confirmed as a "basic component of the European Social Model."[20]

In the speeches and documents associated with the Lisbon meeting, perpetual mobilization (*formation permanente*) was projected as constant, inevitable, and ultimately beneficial for society. The goal of "shaping a new Europe" focused on the importance of the transition to the knowledge economy and on the role of education and training in constituting a new dynamic and competitive European labor force. In this vision the challenge of reformation and retraining was devolved from the responsibility of the state to the agency of individuals, who were expected to choose personally effective learning strategies.

In the rhetoric of globalization, competition, and lifelong learning of that time period there was a strong underlying push for constant personal mobilization and entrepreneurial behavior on the part of individuals, while at the same time the many structural and institutional constraints to achieving these goals were obscured. Further, the inexorable emphasis on the individual and on his or her educational choices constructed rational, atomized agents responsible for their own life paths in lieu of groups or classes experiencing collective dislocation as the result of widespread socioeconomic restructuring under the processes of neoliberal globalization. This accompanied a more general abdication of responsibilities in providing truly viable economic opportunities for workers and/or for the harmonious integration of immigrants and minorities into European society.

Further, the original personal and social development emphasis of lifelong learning as detailed in earlier documents from the 1970s was relegated to a minor rhetorical key. Community funds for lifelong learning went primarily into workplace retraining programs rather than into curricula emphasizing social or civic education such as the study of culture, comparative democracy, or systems of government. Thus, with the transformation of lifelong learning, European social cohesion became advanced more through the formation of a flexible and mobile cross-border labor force than through the notion of personal development and the constitution of democratic participants in society.

In all of these transformations there was a demonstrable effort by elites to shape Europe into the most premier knowledge economy in the world. In EU programs and discourses of the time one can see attempts to construct a fast-paced, mobile, and interchangeable laborer for this knowledge venue. Earlier concerns about the importance of social cohesion, including the emphasis on achieving diversity as beneficial for civic life and for the development of a European community, were replaced or accompanied with economistic assumptions about individual human capital. Moreover, it became the individual's responsibility to integrate effectively. If he or she did not, it was projected as an issue of individual choice rather than the failure of the egalitarian claims of liberalism.

These transformations were broadly linked with macroeconomic shifts relating to late-twentieth-century systems of flexible accumulation and the rise of neoliberalism as a political philosophy of governance. Indeed, the educational directives of the EU during this time did not just line up in accordance with these broader shifts but were in fact key mechanisms in reconstructing governance structures more widely. As the EU expanded through the early 2000s it began to take on a more productive, and some argue greater imperial role in shaping policy, disciplining member states, and forming a European educational space that served as a "division of the neoliberal army."[21]

The educational strategies of this time, as Susan Robertson has noted, began to point towards a European project and vision of global leadership in the production of higher learning and knowledge in the European interest.[22] Knowledge, in this image of the future—for both Europeans and North Americans— required not just the cooperation of choice-making and entrepreneurial individuals and learners, but also the spaces and managerial experts of a brave new society.

Spaces of the Knowledge Economy, Creative Cities, and the New Managerial Elite

When it first appeared in policy and academic discourse, lifelong learning was often coupled with the concepts of the learning society or the knowledge economy. All of these concepts emerged around the same time from scholars in the fields of education and management. These discourses reinforced a mythology that treated knowledge as a social and economic panacea. At the heart of this mythology was the figure of the knowledge worker. Peter Drucker, who coined the term in the 1950s, defined knowledge workers as "accountants, engineers, social workers, nurses, computer experts of all kinds, teachers and researchers," or, more broadly, people "who are paid for putting knowledge to work rather than brawn or manual skill."[23]

In Europe, the lifelong education of knowledge workers and the construction of the so-called knowledge economy could be best conceptualized as a space for new kinds of market opportunities. Both the language and the policies of lifelong learning and the knowledge economy carved out a terrain in which education and work were yoked together in a complex construction of personal value and human capital development, national and transnational community, and territory. This agglomeration provided multiple spaces for capital accumulation.

In the United States, the mythos of knowledge work was grafted onto popular imaginations of urban space through concepts such as the creative city, first pitched in the late 1980s. More recent buzzwords have included "smart city," "learning city," "knowledge city," and "resilient city." The creative city was first discussed in Richard Florida's famous thesis about the rise of the creative class.[24] Florida argued that in the context of deindustrialization and the decline of manufacturing in core countries, knowledge workers were the emergent demographic critical for postindustrial cities to survive (rather than the older demographic segment appropriate for older manufacturing-based economies).

For Florida, the creative class in the United States was an increasingly important and valuable subsection of the workforce. It included a "super-creative core" of occupations focusing on the creative process and problem solving, as well as a group of creative professionals consisting of knowledge-based workers more generally. In the contemporary global economy, according to Florida, this class acted as a major driver of economic growth through its ability to innovate, as well as its ability to be flexible and adapt to changing economic needs. As a result, cities should make every effort to attract these workers. Florida argued that creative types were particularly drawn to cities that fostered cultural values of diversity, openness, and tolerance—in the business realm but also in terms of an artistic and bohemian scene.

Placing such a premium on knowledge work and creativity recast the city as a marketing hub for the promotion of an edgy brand or lifestyle, one that it pitted against other cities in the competition over so-called creative talent. This culture industry was, however, geared towards a very small segment of the working population. Not only did certain cities lose out in the scramble for creative labor, but the elite utopia of the creative city—as it played out in the policies, investment strategies, and development projects installed for attracting and retaining the creative class—tended to intensify urban inequalities along lines of class, gender, and race.

Florida's ideas were extremely persuasive to those urban politicians and institutions struggling to fashion their cities in ways attractive to international capital investment. Creating an urban revival by courting the "hip and cool" was a relatively cheap strategy, and one that urban elites embraced wholeheartedly in the early 2000s. But, as Jamie Peck has shown, the main benefits of this "good business climate" strategy— one of appealing to the most creative members of society through the provision of things like bike lanes, attractive downtown housing, and gay-friendly policies—has flowed primarily to real estate developers and members of the urban elite. It has neither galvanized urban economies nor trickled down to lower-wage workers, as initially conceptualized.[25] Indeed, the strategy actively worked against the interests of the poor and lower-income residents of cities. It often intensified gentrification processes and discouraged the intervention of local governments in providing social services and affordable housing to the insufficiently flexible or "non-creative" members of society.

The global promotion of the knowledge economy and its spatial manifestation in creative cities or a "Europe of tomorrow" policy sphere had widespread and lingering effects beyond economic exclusion. Cultural assumptions about personal worth and the value of certain kinds of work were (and remain) deeply affected by this discourse. As Oakley and O'Brien have noted:

> The workforce of these industries, the "creative class" celebrated by policymakers and depicted as key to economic growth ... is seen to be endowed with particular characteristics—flexibility, adaptability, creativity and even "tolerance"—which are themselves often the product of stratification. To be lacking in these qualities is to be designated as not having value or worth in society.[26]

Oakley and O'Brien demonstrated further how these webs of belief about labor and value played out in schools and in higher education admissions, as well as in cultural labor markets. Moreover, even as admissions directors and urban policy makers made value judgments about worthy students and valued workers, so too did the students and workers themselves.

The effort to become a valued member of society through higher education or lifelong learning, or otherwise joining the ranks of the knowledge economy, is now a global phenomenon, as discussed in Part I. But the success of this effort remains stratified not just by class and other axes of difference, but also by culture itself. In a vicious cycle, the spaces of the knowledge economy and the creative city are linked to certain characteristics of learning, and these in turn are associated with forms of cultural capital attributed to the (largely white, primarily male) middle classes. Even when those of lower social class obtain higher degrees or certificates of advanced learning, they are comparatively disadvantaged in mobilizing these experiences and forms of knowledge to access the labor market. Thus the desired cultural attributes of the knowledge economy and creative city workers—such as creativity and tolerance—continue to advantage the elite even as its promoters suggest the opposite.

Lifelong learning poses as an important path to individual autonomy and freedom as well as economic stability for workers, especially for those who have been displaced by economic restructuring. Yet the same blockages to social mobility that are encountered in more traditional educational pathways remain in place. In this sense, the promotion of creativity, flexibility, and tolerance as necessary characteristics of the "new economy" worker can be seen as something of a red herring—examples of a larger process of depoliticization wherein, despite the liberal patina of change, underlying problems of inequality, immobility, and injustice remain intact. Against the backdrop of the new economy, the latter appear as the products of intolerance or inflexibility. They become issues of psychological or cultural difference—intolerant ways of life—rather than structural imbalances demanding concrete political action.[27]

Whatever its good intentions, the uncritical demand for increasing worker creativity and tolerance fails to acknowledge the historical and geographic exclusions that allow for this new kind of worker to emerge in the first place. Those unable to pick up the torch of flexibility—a single mother, an impoverished teen, a non-native speaker—are demonized as logjams in an otherwise progressive system.

Such paradoxical freedom is most evident in the way the production of knowledge workers has been coupled with an increased need for managing these "autonomous" workers. This is apparent in Drucker's writings on knowledge work. On the one hand, he emphasized how the worker was most productive when unsupervised: "He [sic] must direct, manage and motivate himself."[28] Yet Drucker mentioned elsewhere that a knowledge society "requires ... that knowledge and the knowledge worker be managed productively."[29]

Drucker's ambivalence points to a deeper contradiction within capitalist accumulation, one that becomes very pronounced in a knowledge economy. This is the tension, noted by Marx, between the need to increase the level of cooperation between workers (to increase their productive power) and the need to control this cooperation (to orient it towards the aims of profit). In theory, by bringing workers together in new ways, cooperation produces the conditions for a collective power among labor and thus poses a potential threat to "the domination of power."[30] It is in reaction to the threat of resistance that, for Marx, the role of the modern manager emerges and becomes necessary for continued accumulation—"the work of directing, superintending, and adjusting."[31]

Marx would have found this kind of managerial work even more imperative in a knowledge economy, where the ideal worker is presumably given a larger degree of freedom and autonomy as an entrepreneurial actor in the global market. On the one hand, the dissemination of knowledge as a commodity presupposes a new kind of management style—a form of governance—whereby the worker comes to manage himself or herself in line with the interests of efficiency, flexibility, and the creation of profit. This is a kind of dispossession by possession, in which the worker becomes nudged into norms of productivity through his or her acquisition of mythic "knowledge." Through the commoditization of education, getting ahead in the global economy means working on yourself, acquiring new skills when needed, learning to invest in what the market demands.

At the same time, in line with Marx's arguments about management, the knowledge economy demands external governance as well. Knowledge must be policed and shaped to fit the socket holes of profit. In the United States this is demonstrated by the explosive growth of the managerial and professional classes in recent decades.

The dissemination of "business knowledge" since the 1960s is what Nigel Thrift called the "cultural circuit of capital."[32] Within this cultural circuit—where individual knowledge and economic success become interchangeable concepts—managerial coercion appears natural. Against the linear narrative of consent replacing coercion in the workplace, the management literature on knowledge work suggests that external coercion remains, and even increases, as an important tool for aligning the goals of the worker with those of the firm.

What has changed, as Michael Burawoy has noted, is the extent to which coercion becomes naturalized within the firm and internalized within the individual.[33] Rather than a separate force, coercion appears as the object of consent when the individual chooses to opt in to a system of rules. When knowledge is fetishized as an organizational principle within the firm, the ideal manager acquires the status of an all-knowing guru or visionary leader. It is in this way, as Antonio Gramsci recognized long ago, that knowledge becomes weaponized along class lines as "cultural hegemony."[34] Today, the cultural hegemony of capital serves to empower a managerial class, an elite group of individuals given special access to and mobility across the contours of capitalism.

5

Global Restructuring and Challenges to Citizenship

In the last two chapters I looked at some of the shifts in the values and goals of multiculturalism and lifelong learning at the turn of the twenty-first century. The focus was on social and institutional change in the context of economic transformation, and how new ideas about learning can become dominant in society. However, while powerful entities such as state actors, experts and institutions of various kinds may push a particular vision of education, how other actors—such as school administrators, teachers, parents, and students—react to these policies is equally critical to consider. Moreover, these latter interlocutors produce their own visions and goals, which may or may not accord with those of policy-making politicians and bureaucrats.

The main questions in this chapter thus concern how those most directly impacted by contemporary educational policies and reforms have helped to produce and also adapt to the changing values and aims for education discussed earlier. How have some of the affected populations challenged or accepted assumptions about the need for more strategic types of education for young people, greater flexibility in work training, and/or new understandings of what it means to be an efficient learner or productive citizen? Here I investigate some of the contested transformations in values and subjectivities prevalent in the ongoing mantra of flexibility and entrepreneurialism for the global economy. I look particularly at some of the ways that notions of citizenship and belonging are debated and contested in North America, drawing on a case study from Richmond, a suburb of Vancouver, Canada. In order to give some background to these struggles I first introduce a brief analysis of Western forms of citizenship and some of its cultural meanings and spatial changes over time.

Shifting Scales of Citizenship

In the medieval period a citizen was, by definition, an inhabitant of a city or town, and his location as a townsman conferred on him certain rights.

A few centuries later, the citizen was understood to be a free member of a nation-state. In both of these early usages, the citizen was one who was specifically defined through his (it was a status exclusive to men) location in space—initially as a member of a city, then later as a member of a national community.

In his famous work *Democracy and Education*, John Dewey wrote about the importance of education in the formation of a democratic community.[1] Dewey's work, along with the majority of democratic theorists of the mid-twentieth century, assumed that "community" was inherently and naturally bound within the contours of the nation-state. Indeed, the democratic project that Dewey promoted was explicitly aimed at the formation of the American nation. In his view "America" was to be defined in terms of a shared experience of living and learning together in an open, plural, and egalitarian manner. In this sense, education for democratic citizenship concerned the mutual constitution and development of liberalism, democracy, and the American nation.

Writing at roughly the same time, the British sociologist T.H. Marshall famously delineated three different periods of citizenship formation, beginning with the civil rights of the seventeenth and eighteenth centuries, moving to widening forms of political rights in the nineteenth, and from there to the social rights of the mid-twentieth century.[2] In Marshall's view, citizenship formation followed (and would continue to follow) a positive trajectory of ever-greater inclusiveness and expansiveness with respect to liberal rights and entitlements. Hence, in the first period, citizenship encompassed entitlements such as *habeas corpus* and trial by jury; the second period saw the institutionalization of parliamentary rights and the enfranchisement of white working men (and later African-American men, and women); and the twentieth century era of "social" citizenship included welfare support and subsidies in the areas of health and education—ideally so that individuals could participate in the democratic community despite severe poverty and other deprivations.

While Marshall's insights were helpful in that he recognized the mutability of citizenship, his theory was limited in scope. Writing from his own position in postwar Britain and during a period of strong economic growth and welfare state expansion, he theorized a seemingly natural progression between economic development and the evolution of liberal civil society. His theoretical framework reflected his own hopes that greater political spaces and freedoms (through more expansive understandings and inclusions of citizenship) would open up for everyone as a matter of course alongside economic growth and widening policies of state redistribution.

These political freedoms and rights, however, had always expanded alongside systemic forms of socioeconomic inequality rooted in the development and advance of capitalism. For liberal thinkers such as Marshall and Dewey, this type of disjuncture was a historical problem, one that would inevitably be resolved through greater economic redistribution and the extension of citizenship to more regions and populations. But for radical scholars, citizenship's seemingly contradictory origins and early development (that is, expanding political freedoms developing in conjunction with growing economic inequalities) was hardly an accident of history; rather, the expansion of citizenship manifested state technologies of management and control underpinning deliberate ruling-class strategies within a capitalist system.

Michael Mann, for example, emphasized the origins and development of citizenship in relation to class, arguing that citizenship functioned as a form of governance upholding inequitable economic conditions and hierarchical social relations.[3] For him, the political freedoms of citizenship and national belonging were integral to capitalist forms of social reproduction. Although this was an important thesis, Mann neglected the strong racial and spatial implications of his argument— specifically the important dimensions of state territoriality and national allegiance as well as various kinds of racialized bordering practices. For example, in terms of managing "unruly" populations at home— through the subordination and/or incorporation of immigrants, ethnic minorities, and indigenous groups—the creation of citizenship also helped to create sociocultural, as well as political-economic, boundaries of belonging and nationalism.[4]

These practices of social stratification by race and ethnicity operated (and continue to operate in many ways) within the borders of the nation-state, creating exclusive forms of both legal and cultural citizenship that create an inside and an outside vis-à-vis national belonging. Liberal conceptions of citizenship were also exclusionary with respect to colonies and white-settler societies. The "natives" could be excluded from the liberal rights and freedoms then expanding in Britain and other liberal Western societies through projecting ideas of childishness and irrationality onto those being colonized.[5]

Cultural Citizenship and Contested Belonging

Citizenship's conceptualization in terms of the experience of social belonging and solidarity is often referred to as cultural citizenship. Cultural citizenship embodies processes of self-making but it also reflects the multiple forces that act on cultural subjectivity—many of them both spatial and racial, as indicated above. In the contemporary period, Aihwa Ong has located the formative processes of cultural citizenship in relation to transnational capitalism and the ways that diasporic Asian immigrants, in particular, are frequently positioned vis-à-vis their economic status, country of origin, and race. Status and access reflect economic privilege but also the forms of racialization operative in the host society at a given time or place. Depending on their economic status, immigrants can be "whitened" or "blackened" by the host society—as either model minorities or unassimilable others.[6]

Cultural citizenship formation in the current period manifests shifting scales and processes of belonging. These more fluid and disembedded types of social relations and practices—sometimes referred to as processes of "deterritorialization"—raise important questions about the contemporary formation of a democratic society of citizens.[7] Democratic participation within communities formerly defined by a distinct, national territory has clearly changed as global movements and economic restructuring have disrupted normative assumptions about the nation-state as the primary scale of citizenship and belonging.

These challenges to national primacy, however, are often bitterly contested and frequently contradictory. For example, government policies aimed at encouraging people to be more mobile, flexible, and globally competent discussed in previous chapters came from multiple state and suprastate actors and institutions. Yet as Parker has showed with respect to the push for more International Education schools in the United States during this same period, these exhortations were often simultaneously (and paradoxically) promoted alongside ongoing nationalist expectations for greater domestic economic competitiveness and military readiness.[8] Moreover, while the push for international education and global economic competence is narrated as including everyone, only certain individuals and populations are actually able or willing to consent to these types of fast-paced global "opportunities."

Lower-income, immigrant, and minority groups often remain trapped in poor quality, segregated neighborhoods and schools and, if able to move internationally at all, are detained and harassed at national borders. In these ways the actual conditions for more flexible cross-border movements and access to the knowledge economy and flexible forms of citizenship are extremely limited. Correspondingly, who can demand or choose different learning venues, and who is able to take advantage—or not—of global opportunities for transnational mobility is contingent on the dynamics of race, gender, and class as well as of existing citizenship statuses and national power and prestige.

Well aware of these differentiations of power and global access, people seek to fashion their own strategies for survival and educational success. Thus, while it is important to investigate the ways in which the state attempts to construct new relationships to capital mobility through the figure of the lifelong learner or strategic cosmopolitan, it is also imperative to look at how people fashion themselves. In the contemporary period these self-fashioning strategies and demands for certain kinds of schools and employment opportunities reflect the subject positions and identities of individuals and populations as they seek to find a place in a changing economy and society.

In her book *Flexible Citizenship*, Ong examined the particular practices and strategies of transnational Chinese subjects as they engaged with the changes brought about by global capitalism at the turn of the twenty-first century. Her focus was on the everyday lives and imaginings that were central to "the condition of cultural interconnectedness and mobility across space" of this population.[9] She looked specifically at those who operated in flexible cross-border arrangements of various kinds— through migration, business networks, and familial ties.

Through studying the everyday practices and imaginings of this diasporic population, Ong contended that she could provide a more substantial analysis of the dynamics of globalization and flexible forms of capitalist accumulation than those of what she perceived to be overly structuralist accounts. In her view, ethnographic methods that pay attention to human agency provide the best glimpse into the workings of global capitalism. She found that the cosmopolitan Chinese subjects of her study navigated the contours of a new global order and reacted to its transformative processes, but that they also produced changes in its functioning through their own culturally informed ideas and practices. In this view the meaning of citizenship is never completely fixed in stone: it is a status, an ideology, a feeling, and a set of practices that are constantly challenged and re-formed on an ongoing basis, including through struggles over education.

In the next section I investigate some of these ideas through a study of schools in Richmond, a suburb of Vancouver, British Columbia, on the west coast of Canada. I examine strong differences of opinion over what public education systems should provide. The struggle over Richmond's schools took place in the context of global transformation and rapid cultural and economic changes brought about by large-scale immigration from Hong Kong in the 1980s and 1990s. This migration into Vancouver accelerated rapidly owing to new "business" and "investor" categories in the Canadian immigration process that facilitated the entry of wealthy immigrants. Many of these business migrants came because of the pending transition of Hong Kong to sovereign control by China in 1997.

The lines of battle over education in Richmond were drawn primarily between white Canadian residents and recent Hong Kong Chinese immigrants. The former group fought for a more child-centered educational system along the lines that Dewey had advocated. Good citizenship education, in their view, involved learning to tolerate and encourage individual and group differences in the spirit of Canadian multiculturalism. The Chinese group, by contrast, promoted a more traditional, disciplined, "back to basics" type of education for children, one that emphasized skills-based learning, greater standardization and accountability, and a more hierarchical, teacher-centered approach. Becoming a good citizen, for this group, was more related to academic achievement and respect for authority.

In this study some key elements to note include the global political, economic, and spatial transformations that parents were reacting to and struggling over; the uneven reception of and reaction to these larger forces depending on their identities and subject positions; and the ways in which ideas and practices related to education, citizenship, and work were discussed and contested. Most important, through these struggles, new beliefs and political formations were collectively produced.

Traditional Schools in Richmond

At the end of the 1990s there were three types of school choice in British Columbia: state-funded schools, independent or private schools, and home schooling. Within the state education system, however, "alternative schools" represented another layer of school choice. Although they were government funded, alternative schools could have their own focus and mission statement and could offer specialized programs such as French immersion or the International Baccalaureate. Among the group of alternative schools in British Columbia were Montessori, fine arts, career and technical centers, and so-called "traditional" schools.

At the time, local school boards had the power to develop alternative programs for the district, and generally did so in response to public pressure. In 1999 there were five traditional schools operating in British Columbia, three of which were established in the 1980s by parents with a strong Christian fundamentalist background. Each of these schools had slightly varying programs under the general banner of "back to basics" or "fundamental" education. One definition of fundamental education culled from the traditional school proposals and the available literature included the following features: an emphasis on the basics of reading, writing, and arithmetic; phonic drills, memorization, and consistent homework assignments; moral or character development, including respect for authority; highly controlled pupil behavior (reflected in policies such as uniforms and strict disciplinary sanctions); teacher-centered instructional methods; and high levels of competition through the use of standardized tests.[10]

Since the alternative schools had to follow the same basic curriculum as state-funded neighborhood schools, traditional schools were differentiated less on the basis of their instructional focus than on their general atmosphere, particularly the emphasis on competition, parental and teacher authority, and on the inculcation of a strict, moral code. Studies of traditional schools in British Columbia showed that the primary differences between traditional and neighborhood schools existed in a higher level of parental involvement in traditional schools, as well as a greater emphasis on authority, and in the strong coordination of values and learning between home and school.

The first proposal to open a traditional school in Richmond was voted down by the School Board in a six-to-one vote in 1996. At the time of the vote, the School Board was composed primarily of teachers with left-of-center political affiliations to such organizations as the British Columbia Teacher's Federation and the New Democratic Party. Over the next two years, however, there was a shift in the composition of the School Board toward a more conservative political membership. At the same time, there was a campaign by members of the district to promote the traditional school proposal. On June 15, 1998, a newly configured board voted four to three to support further feasibility studies for a new traditional school, with a likely opening date in fall 1999. What happened in the two years between 1996 and 1998 is an important indicator of the shifts in community dynamics in Richmond, and in the perception of and conflicts over the philosophy and practice of education, work, and citizenship in Canadian society during this time.

Joanne Fischer, a white Canadian, proposed opening the traditional school in 1996, but the vast majority of support in the years between 1996 and 1998 came from recent Chinese-Canadian immigrants to Richmond. One of the galvanizing moments for this latter group occurred during a Chinese-language radio talk show hosted by Hanson Lau, a resident who had arrived from Hong Kong two decades earlier. On his show, Lau hosted John Pippus, an outspoken traditional-school proponent. He asked his listeners to indicate interest in the establishment of another traditional school by phoning the radio station. Lau received 70 calls from Chinese parents, and followed this up by arranging for them to meet with Pippus and learn the process of setting up a traditional school in their own neighborhoods.

In the year following the radio show there was a blitz of information, discussion, public meetings, editorials and letters to the editor of the local paper, the *Richmond News*, all related to the proposed traditional school in Richmond and to the meaning and practices of education more generally. At public hearings convened by the School Board, between 100 and 200 people spoke vociferously for the proposal. School Board presidents reported receiving numerous phone calls at their homes prior to meetings and decisions, and the *Richmond News* received multiple letters to the editor.

In one of these letters, written by May Leung, a recent Chinese immigrant in 1998, some of the differing conceptualizations of the meanings and practices of education were immediately apparent:

> We came to this lovely city five years ago. After spending half of our wealth settling down here. Our children were registered into the neighborhood school under the public [i.e. state-funded] school system and curriculum. We were so pleased to be here ... But after a while, everything turned into a nightmare. The economy is down and falling, and worst of all, our children's performances are much lower both in academic and moral areas. I noticed the children have learnt very little academically. They learned to have self-confidence

instead of being self-disciplined; learned to speak-up instead of being humbled; learned to be creative instead of self-motivated; and learned to simplify things instead of organizing. All of these characteristics were not balanced, and will be the source of disadvantage and difficulties in children in this competitive society ... It is time to change, because it is our children who face the future. They should be better equipped and I think "traditional" schooling would help them to build a solid ground.[11]

This letter was followed by a number of scathing responses in the same newspaper. The following is one of the many reactions to May Leung's and other letters that were written in support of the proposal for a traditional school in Richmond:

May Leung sets out the case for "traditional" schools more succinctly than most in her May 13 letter. She wants her children to be self-disciplined, humble, self-motivated and organized, instead of being self-confident, assertive, creative and analytical ... These repressive, authoritarian "traditional" parents who hanker for the days of yore, when fresh-faced school kids arrived all neatly decked out in drab-grey uniforms and shiny lace-up leather shoes, are a menace to society. They desire their kids to sit quietly in tidy serried ranks while Teech, in gown and mortar board, drills them relentlessly in their ABCs and times tables. Should they err in any way, a thousand lines or a good beating will learn 'em real good. Give 'em chalk and talk, make 'em learn by rote, have 'em regurgitate scads of Wordsworth and Formulae on demand and test the little dears weekly. That's the order of the day. If it was good enough for us, it must be good for them, mustn't it? Stands to reason, after all. The world has changed, and the education system with it. No longer do we have grinding production lines or clerk-filled office blocks ready to receive the output from scholastic factories, tutored to be polite, obliging little cyphers complying with the whims of magisterial management. Such humble folk have been down-sized onto the dole in the interests of globalization and the next quarter's bottom line.[12]

A number of key themes are apparent in the initial letter and the response. The recently arrived émigré, May Leung, desired an ethical code within the school system, one that would ensure that her children were "well equipped" to live and work efficiently within an increasingly "competitive" society. It was a position validating achievement, organization, and authority over the assertive but potentially inefficient and disorganized individual. Leung's position was denounced by long-term residents of the neighborhood, who asserted a child's right to be individualistic and nonconformist.

The idea of an individual child's right to be different was also extended to a discussion of broader social differences such as those based on class or special needs. Many respondents in the newspapers and in interviews suggested that advocates of traditional schools reflected a desire to return to a perceived era of order and efficiency that, by its nature, excluded a number of so-called unassimilable individuals and social groups. They felt that the stated traditional-school emphasis on same-age groups, the tracking of the brightest students, uniforms, morals, tests, and strict consistency in teaching and homework indicated a desire for classrooms of children who were essentially alike. Children who were different because of their family background, learning abilities or style, or just because of individual quirkiness, would not fit into this type of school. One respondent wrote, for example:

> The advocates of "traditional" schools are trying to recreate the past, a past that did not include recognition of individual differences, differing levels of English understanding, the mentally and physically challenged and the new world of computer technology among other things … Aside from the monetary cost of even the research into such a change to the system, the division in our society which would be created would separate our citizens into "classes"—a type of society which my father and many other people came to Canada to escape. Minority pressure groups should not be allowed to use public money to alter a system that has taken years to develop. We must look to the future, not the past.[13]

The perspectives expressed in these letters represent just a few of the many positions taken in the debate over the opening of the traditional school in Richmond.[14] Yet in many respects these views represented some of the key differences emerging between the longer-term white residents and the more recent Chinese immigrants with regard to the discussion of educational practice and philosophy. These philosophical differences led to the mobilization of an activist and powerful ethnic community around the issue of education. They also led to real political and educational changes in Richmond within a relatively short time period.

After the School Board decision to initiate a feasibility study of the proposal for a traditional school in June 1998, a sixteen-person committee was formed to discuss the issue further. This committee met ten times between July and February that year and decided to introduce many of the changes demanded by the proponents of traditional schools to all the schools in Richmond. Instead of opening one traditional school, which committee members felt "by default … could become a school populated only by Chinese children," the committee recommended that the board adopt many of the traditional-school suggestions for all schools in the district. Otherwise, according to the chair of the committee, "If the majority of the students are Chinese, how are they going to learn English? Also, how are we going to encourage them to get into the mainstream? It's not subscribing to the multicultural philosophy of the community."[15]

The two key recommendations for change identified by the committee were increased communication between school and home, and greater consistency in practice (across schools and across grades within the same school). Following the committee's recommendations, Chris Kelly, superintendent of the Richmond school district, decided to establish a Foundations Program for Richmond schools. He initiated the process with a series of public meetings between administrators, parents, and teachers. The purpose of the meetings was to begin a dialogue about educational practice and pedagogic philosophy.

At the second meeting, which I attended on May 11, 1999, the conversation at one table focused on children's learning.[16] One woman who had migrated recently from Hong Kong, but who was not a major proponent of traditional schools, said that the main concern of Hong Kong Chinese parents was the sense that there was no way to assess their child's progress through the school year or in comparison with other children. She claimed that many Chinese parents were frustrated by the lack of standardized textbooks, the small amount of homework required of children, and the lack of standardized testing.[17] In Hong Kong, by contrast, tests were administered at least once a month in order to evaluate the student's progress, and parents were required to go over large amounts of homework with the child every night. Most homework, moreover, was taken directly from chapters in a textbook that was used consistently in all classes in Hong Kong at that grade level.

The two Richmond schoolteachers at the table replied to this information by arguing that strict standardization and consistency in classes and across schools were not conducive to learning as a process. One teacher said:

> children learn in different ways. One size does not fit all. All children are different and each child can and must learn differently. Learning is not episodic but a process, where some things may not be learned right away but over time.

The recently arrived migrant said that Chinese parents feared that, with different evaluation structures, a child might fall behind and neither the parents nor the child would be aware of it. She said that ongoing and standardized assessment is part of the communication process, how parents know where the child is in terms of his or her level. Another teacher responded to this by noting that constant comparison with other children is problematic since parents then measure success by what other children accomplish rather than their child's own learning progress. The first teacher added: "competition is the problem. It comes into conflict with many ways of knowing."

This meeting adjourned after the superintendent discussed a number of ways to introduce some of the learning foundations discussed at the meetings into the classrooms of selected elementary schools in Richmond. These new foundations were based on the themes of clarity, consistency and communication between teachers, parents, and students. They were initiated in a handful of schools in September 1999 and then extended to all schools in the Richmond district the following year.

In the Richmond study, the majority of Chinese immigrants were supportive of a more skills-based education with more standardized testing. For some of these parents, greater standardization offered the possibility of more educational portability in the case of a transnational move, but also a greater ability to benchmark their child's progress against others. This indicated an economic concern about competition and falling behind in the race to global market success. But it also reflected concerns about communication—a lack of knowledge and awareness about how the system worked and how to gauge a child's development within it.

More rules and regulations, more memorization, standardization, and accountability were felt to provide a better communicative system and a more consistent or "level" playing field. Without this type of structure, recent migrants felt a lack of access to cultural citizenship—a form of belonging and solidarity with the political community, but one also implicitly connected with economic integration and access. Educating for citizenship, in these parents' view, was equated with a structure of learning that focused on cultural belonging through academic success, a form of success made accessible via standardized systems of education.

Meanwhile, most white Richmond residents held onto a sense of education for citizenship predicated on engaging individual differences and different (non-standardized) ways of learning. This emphasis on engaging and celebrating difference was also implicitly linked with what it meant to be a tolerant, liberal thinker, and a Canadian. At the micro scale, the struggle was over pedagogy—what is the best way for children to learn? But in the context of transnational movements and market capitalism it was far more complicated than this. The different opinions reflected the differing subject positions of class, race, and nationality during this time period, and the ways in which these forms of identity and status influenced conceptions of democratic community and what education should do and be.

The promulgation of tolerance of difference—the philosophy of liberal multiculturalism—can be seen in this larger context as a form of governance. Rather than engaging with broader questions of cultural citizenship and the inability of non-white immigrants to access the forms of cultural belonging promoted by Canadian schools, the discussion over learning turned on questions of difference and tolerance. As Wendy Brown has noted, the language of tolerance often serves to depoliticize discussion, redirecting claims of equity, entitlement, and belonging to the domain of identity and respect.[18] While arguing for tolerance and respect for difference, white Canadians upheld normative assumptions that function over the long term to privilege and advantage certain kinds of local knowledge and cultural and economic capital and exclude others.

At the same time, the recently arrived Chinese immigrants were not naïve or passive dupes of ideology. They actively sought to intervene in a system they felt was not working to their advantage. Employing a different rhetoric, that of preparation for the global economy, the parents countered one dominant narrative with another. In doing so they became active participants in the struggle over public education and how students should be constituted as successful workers and citizens in the neoliberal era.

This case study manifests some of the ironies and contradictions of the millennial moment. It might be expected that Chinese migrants to Vancouver, who have experienced great racial discrimination historically in that city, would be ardent supporters of liberal multiculturalism. Yet in the battle over state-funded education in the suburban Richmond school district, this was not the case. Factors such as class position played a role in this outcome. So too did the historical and geographical context.

My aim in introducing this research was to highlight the agency of individual actors and the multiple, divergent, and often contradictory responses to educational policies and assumptions in any given context. How different groups and individuals react to, engage with, and help produce those assumptions reflects their own identities and socioeconomic positions. In the next part of the book I introduce some key recent actors and institutions currently active in the production of critical concepts and policies in education.

PART III

The Reform Coalition

6

Market Philanthropy in Education

In the first part of this book I looked at some of the geographical processes of neoliberal globalization as they impact education systems, social values, and philosophies of learning. As noted, these transformations do not arise in a vacuum. They are part of broader restructuring forces also impacting cities, nations, and the global community. Moreover, in the context of the increasing adoption of *laissez-faire* market systems, the shifts towards more entrepreneurial and competitive modes of operation are becoming embedded in social life itself.

The contemporary era of *Homo economicus* is not a "natural" evolution of liberal thought or economic life, however. It has come about because of very deliberate choices made by specific sets of actors. Examining some of these actions, situated within particular times and places, gives us a sense of how neoliberalism has emerged and taken shape in the way that it has. This, in turn, enables a better view of the practices of actors currently active in education today.

Over the past decade a new set of elite actors has become increasingly influential in education politics. Prominent among these are the founders of philanthropic foundations and the directors of social-impact investment funds. In the United States the most influential foundations include the Bill and Melinda Gates Foundation, the Eli and Edythe Broad Foundation, and the Walton Family Foundation. These, along with many others, are currently investing hundreds of millions of dollars in various kinds of education reform projects throughout the country. Although not yet as influential on the education scene, there are also a number of new actors and institutions with similar ideas about catalyzing reform in the education sectors in England and Canada.

Before examining a few of the specific aims and effects of these reforms it is worth analyzing some of the broader rationales for education investment in the first place. This takes us back to a contextual investigation of the development of liberal capitalism and the rise of neoliberalism in the twentieth century, and the problems of government and market failure that many foundations seek to address. Once again, there is a geographical component to this.

Market ideologies and practices evolve depending on the conditions of implementation in specific milieus, and thus the form that liberalism has taken over the past century looks quite different in different times and places. One of the key advantages of a geographical perspective is highlighting and foregrounding this kind of context. In his book *Constructions of Neoliberal Reason*, for example, Jamie Peck conducted a spatial genealogy of the rise of neoliberalism and its uneven spread across the globe.[1] He showed how ideas about neoliberal forms of governance were not fixed concepts that were set in stone by Chicago School economists such as Friedrich von Hayek and Milton Friedman or by thought collectives such as the Mont Pèlerin Society. The different locales in which these ideas emerged and developed—and the ways in which they were challenged and resisted—allowed for divergent neoliberal "constructions" across space and time. Peck argued that existing neoliberalism thus manifested (and continues to show) disconnected and even contradictory practices rather than a single, monolithic form.

Geographical research such as this indicates that it is critical to investigate the incomplete and contingent development processes through which neoliberal thinkers, beliefs, and practices continue to cogenerate one another. Often we can see that certain ideas and methods are experimental, temporary, and/or even seem to fail in their original intent or implementation. But it can be exactly these types of temporary pilot projects and failures that produce new strategies of governance. Failures as well as successes can be transformed into knowledge and circulated among practitioners and policy makers.

This is important to think about in terms of how workers are made and education reforms are conceptualized and carried out because in the arena of education policy and practice a new set of powerful and increasingly influential actors has emerged in recent years. Moreover, these philanthropic actors are influencing how neoliberal forms of globalization and economic restructuring are developing in the United States and globally.

These new actors and partnerships have helped to form what Matthew Sparke and I have termed "the new Washington consensus," a power base that is emerging from centers such as the state of Washington—the location of the Gates Foundation.[2] These formations have not supplanted the "old" Washington consensus, a term denoting the importance of

Washington, DC-based politics and persuasion in the arena of economic development. US forms of institutional power—vis-à-vis the World Bank, the International Monetary Fund, and other engines of global development—remains strong. Nevertheless, the Gates Foundation and other private foundations are quickly becoming key nodal points in these power webs.

Philanthropic actors are the new rich of the twenty-first century who now wish to disperse their vast fortunes. They are the wealthiest of the wealthy, men and women (though mostly men) who made money primarily from postindustrial activities: computers, patents, telecommunications, insurance, finance, and real estate. How and where they made their wealth is relevant because the foundations they establish themselves are oriented towards the same kind of business logic that was effective for their founders. This includes considerations of intellectual copyright, targeted and short-term financial investment and leveraging, pilot trials, quick exits, and rapid returns on investment.

In the current neoliberal period the role of these philanthropists and their way of thinking about social investment has been critical for the development of education. This is particularly true in the United States, but this type of thinking is also starting to have an impact in many other Western societies as well, including England and Canada. These social impact investors are intervening in the "business" of education (as well as other areas such as health) because of perceived failures in the provision of decent quality education by the government. In many cases, the philanthropists have also noted the obvious failures of the market in providing adequate housing, health care, and education for the poorest segments of society. Through their foundations, they want to make a difference, but the fixes they promote emphasize quasi-private or public–private partnerships and ideas, many of which rely on the same market forces that failed or were insufficient in addressing these problems from the start.

The public–private partnerships (PPPs) most often advocated are between organizations such as private foundations, the government, and various other non-profit and for-profit institutions and players. The money given or loaned by philanthropic ventures in education is often used to catalyze and/or leverage other funds, and is generally expected to have either a financial or social return on investment.

Paralleling the rise of these new market-oriented actors and partnerships is a growing reliance on business logics and language.

This has become a dominant motif, not just in education, but also in many other PPP realms. More and more frequently one hears terms in everyday life that used to resonate primarily in the business world. In addition to "24/7," "quick fix," and "return on investment," these include language such as "benchmarking," "best practices," and "evidence-based policy." Additionally, because of the interlinkages and connections between public and private realms, PPPs are ultimately dependent on market-friendly policies in the arena of contracts, intellectual copyright, and labor management.

While assessment and accountability have always been an important part of rigorous education systems, in recent years the push to be accountable and assess everything more frequently has grown exponentially. Students are assessed not just on their coursework but also on their overall levels of development in all areas of the curriculum. Meanwhile, teachers are assessed regarding the achievements or failures of their students, principals are assessed for the overall standing of the school, and the district is assessed based on how many schools under its jurisdiction are succeeding or failing. Moreover, metrics-based forms of assessment—measurements that can be quantitatively "benchmarked" against others based on numbers—are emphasized.

These trends towards greater assessment and accountability are associated with the reform coalition in education and the rationale of PPP funding, but they are also indicators of wider trends of neoliberal transformation. The push to standardized testing and accountability is in part because the business logic of human capital development, entrepreneurial behavior, and return on investment—central motifs of neoliberalism—have now infiltrated social as well as economic institutions.

That economic concerns have become central in all aspects of life is problematic because it reduces forms of human sociality to calculative measurements of costs and benefits as well as instrumental assumptions about "return." Moreover, in order to generate social and financial returns, it is necessary to know exactly what those returns are. Metrics therefore form a key component of this narrative, as social "value" must be assessed and assessable in order to calculate a financial return. But the measurement of social returns, such as one finds in education, is not always straightforward.

For example, how does one measure the growth and development of a student's sense of self-worth, love of literature, belief in democratic participation, or respect for the environment? Are there ways to measure and benchmark feelings of tolerance and kindness towards others? While these subjective assessments have always been outside normative systems of measurement in most schools, they could be accorded value in informal ways through teachers and social relationships. The high-stakes testing culture renders these forms of social return of less value because more calculative metrics take over the time and consciousness of school actors.

Despite these difficulties, assumptions about the value of data-oriented efficiencies and the accuracy of accountability metrics enables both philanthropists and political and economic elites in the United States and Europe to use the rationale of science to point government and its multiple partners toward market-oriented solutions to social problems in education. The logic of metrics gains authority through the discourse of neutrality and efficiency. These are often situated positively in relation to an unhindered market system, and in opposition to the alleged biases and blockages associated with horizontal systems of social provision such as through government. The following section investigates the derivation of some of these ideas in older systems of charitable giving, how they have developed more recently in the educational arena, and how, despite claims of neutrality through numbers, they are always striated by race and gender.

Human Capital Development in Philanthropy

In some significant respects, millennial philanthropy resembles early-twentieth-century philanthropic practices, with similar ideas about cost-effectiveness, efficient dispersal of funds, top-down deployment of technical solutions, as well as moral arguments about the rights of human beings to live educated and productive lives. Human capital development has always been a key theme of modern philanthropies. Carnegie and Rockefeller, much like contemporary philanthropists, sought to apply business principles to their private foundations, leveraging their big business reputations and networks as well as introducing strategies designed to maximize human potential in ways they saw as rational. Similarly, they addressed problems of social dysfunction with bold plans for solving them by tying the socially marginalized to the opportunities offered by the marketplace.

Yet these supposedly rational plans for human capital development were racially differentiated from the very beginning. African-Americans, for example, were recipients of targeted and delimited philanthropic donations to education in the American South since the founding of many northern foundations. From the first post-Reconstruction schools and the formation of historically black institutions in the South, up through contemporary educational reforms in inner city neighborhoods, private foundations have been at the forefront of providing funding and making decisions about "appropriate" educational institutions and curricula for African-Americans.[3]

Carnegie, for example, took pains to fund the industrial-model "Negro" colleges Hampton and Tuskegee rather than the more expansive liberal arts colleges Fisk and Lincoln. This was part of a deliberate strategy to keep African-Americans tied to agricultural and factory forms of labor, as well as to mollify post-Reconstruction southerners who wished to circumscribe the possibilities of black achievement in other areas. Similarly, Rockefeller, a believer in social Darwinism and a proponent of the Efficiency Movement, empowered his General Education Board to channel funding in a manner such that "the Negro" would never be "educated out of his environment ... at trades and on the land."[4] These are just a few examples of the countless ways that private northern funders and foundations tried to proscribe and delimit what, where, and how black children and adults should learn.

While many of these methods of differentiated targeting of low-income, women, and minority populations continue in new forms, there are also some critically important differences between the earlier era and the millennial moment. Even more strongly than in previous eras, most current foundations emphasize individual responsibility and choice in the development of the individual's own human potential. The focus is on providing the opportunities and the expert knowledge for people to "lift themselves" out of their own social and economic difficulties so that they can be better integrated into all facets of global capitalist life.[5] This emphasis reflects the neoliberal rationalities discussed earlier: that with the provision of the right tools and incentives, individuals can make the appropriate cost–benefit calculations to better their own circumstances. Furthermore, these calculations are almost always oriented towards greater inclusion in global capitalist markets. Here the philanthropies and their partners—including, but not limited to, government—have the responsibility to incentivize the individual's entrepreneurial capabilities and link them to the global market's vaunted opportunities.

As in the earlier era, individuals in the contemporary moment are also recruited into more active partnering positions in the funding process. Yet this is less in the sense of preparation as productive workers and national citizens as in Carnegie's era, but more as calculating global consumers and entrepreneurs. As partners rather than grantees, recipients of foundation support are made responsible for their behavior and their choices as they are simultaneously invited to share in the foundation's entrepreneurial ideals. The largest contemporary foundations thus exert a top-down, yet simultaneously bottom-up type of pressure on policy through individual recruitment and orientation as well as through funding, networking, and leveraging at all scales of governance.

In the context of these changes it is not surprising that an emergent ethos of everyday survival and program management has been imported from the world of finance. This is the ethos of risk management. Whereas in older forms of philanthropy the rhetorical commitment was to provide funds for tackling the causes of risk, that ideal is now gone. Risk is to be seen as an ongoing feature of the market and hence of life itself. Moreover, risk is now devolved to the grantees or to other partners such as the government, which is expected to share or absorb the risk. While Carnegie's vision of returning the gift of money to "the masses" was a national and more material circuit of wealth generation, the contemporary logic is post-national and dematerialized through the circuits of global financialization.

The Omidyar Network, established by the eBay founder Pierre Omidyar, is a good example of this general trend. The group invests actively in for-profit as well as non-profit ventures and expects to make money in the process. The eBay founder's main concern is that most investors are "too risk-averse" and thus miss the potential—for profit and for social betterment—of working with the so-called bottom billion, the very poorest populations around the world. Omidyar's network has hence backed numerous microfinance initiatives such as Kiva and SKS, which are designed to help those who would otherwise be left out of the presumed advantages of the risk-taking and potential return of global credit in market-based systems.

These types of initiatives have been well documented in the geographical literature, which shows, among other things, the ways that certain populations in the United States and around the globe are identified for risk-taking recruitment. Poor women, in particular, are seen as the perfect agents of individual responsibility and entrepreneurial behavior as they are perceived as more likely to work hard and to repay the investment than men in similar economic circumstances.[6]

Similar in many ways to the previous round of so-called "scientific" philanthropic funding of African-American schools in the US South by Carnegie and Rockefeller, philanthropic capital now is targeted toward specific populations with the intent of inclusion in a broader project of economic insertion in the global economy. It is an intention, however, suffused with the desire and expectation of return—in the first case vis-à-vis northern industrial development and national economic expansion. In more recent iterations, the expectation of return is with respect to a post-national project of global inclusion, as well as social and financial profitability.

Both microfinance and contemporary philanthropy thus operate at a personal as well as a structural level. The competitive and calculative practices foster a market orientation among philanthropic grantees, many of whom are marginalized by race and gender as well as by poverty. Through the process of obtaining funding and through funded projects themselves, recipients are encouraged to see the choices offered by the market as solutions to patriarchy, xenophobia, racism, or other social ills that may beset them. Moreover, through the management-of-funds and return-on-investment mind-set, they are recruited to operate as agents who can become responsible for their own care.

These projects are constantly monitored, and the recipients themselves are expected to submit to the culture of measurement and the metrics of return. Evidence-based investment is imagined as post-political, being strongly associated with ideas of moving beyond the inherent corruption, limitations, borders, and biases of government. Among the perceived limitations of the past was the orientation of Keynesian liberalism in the postwar period. Rather than return to the more nationally mediated regime of Fordism, the current period takes market discipline to new scales. It orients locales and individuals to global, market-based solutions using a calculus of quantitative evidence as well as a purported freedom from the oppression and subordination of previous racist and patriarchal regimes.

Assessment and the Cult of Accountability

Low literacy rates and other negative student outcomes evident in many American public schools, especially in poor and minority neighborhoods, have been highly publicized over the past few decades. But despite a large body of scholarship on the inequitable geographies of resource allocation, income, nutritional and dental health, and other systemic forms of disparity, these negative outcomes are rarely laid at the door of widespread impoverishment and racism.[7] The reputed failure of state-funded schools that is trumpeted by education reformers and their well-funded allies in government and private foundations is not located in structural issues. Rather, it is more frequently represented as deriving from deficiencies such as poorly trained or inadequate teachers, large and overly bureaucratic schools and unions, and the lack of modern technology and modern approaches to contemporary global issues.

The proposed market-oriented solutions to the narrative of state school risk, failure, and crisis do not therefore address concerns of racism or a more generalized neoliberal abandonment. They point towards more superficial and seemingly solvable problems. These involve several components, including more standardized curricula and testing for students; greater teacher accountability, with "evidence-based" assessment tied to tenure, promotion, and termination; more flexibility in the hiring and firing of teachers; and the linkage of federal and local funding for schools to the results of standardized tests.

The strong desire for educational reform based on the principles of assessment and accountability emerged at the federal level in the United States with the No Child Left Behind (NCLB) Act of 2001. This legislative bill was a long time coming, however. In many ways it grew out of the broader context of the negative 1983 report on public schools, "A Nation at Risk," and the growing promulgation of neoliberal market rule under the Reagan presidency.[8] The logic of the "market knows best" was given a somewhat friendlier face during the 1990s under the "third way" regime of Bill Clinton, but it continued just the same.

Educational reforms during the 1990s took place primarily at the city and district levels, including a number of pilot projects that would be immediately heralded, copied, and transferred to other areas of the country. Among these wildly proclaimed reforms was the so-called District Two project on "balanced literacy," a New York City innovation that caught the eye of reformers and was subsequently taken up and mandated for the entire San Diego school district. The main features of this reform included a uniform method of teaching reading, more time spent in the classroom on literacy, and a major expansion of time and money for professional development so that teachers could learn this method and adapt it for their own classrooms.

In her book *The Death and Life of the Great American School System*, Diane Ravitch explored how many of these early educational reforms, including "balanced literacy," were not necessarily bad in and of themselves—indeed, many were commended by researchers and celebrated by progressive politicians—but their implementation was deeply problematic.[9] In San Diego, for example, the entire system was reorganized in short order, with many staff moved or replaced without consultation, 600 classroom aides fired, a new "blueprint" teaching document installed and heavily policed, and school decision-making rescinded. Teacher, principal, and even parent input throughout all of these major transformations was disdained and ignored.

The style of implementation of these early reforms is important because it indicates the shifting attitude towards those most intimately connected with how schools operate and students learn: principals and teachers. In short, Ravitch laid out in careful detail how a highly authoritarian, business-style logic and set of practices crept into the system of public education during the 1980s and 1990s and began to undermine principals, deskill and demoralize teachers, and deracinate the foundations of democracy. This strong authoritarian turn toward reform at all costs, often made in the name of closing the achievement gap and in the spirit of social justice for low-income and minority students, was facilitated and encouraged with funding from the Carnegie, Broad, Gates, and Hewlett foundations, among others.

These rapidly accelerating changes in leadership style at the city and district levels were ushered in at the same moment, and with the same underpinning business logic, as the emphasis on evidence-based assessment, benchmarking, and accountability at the national scale. This was most fully realized with the federal intervention of NCLB, which mandated yearly standardized testing of children in grades three to eight (ages 9 to 13) in every school district in the country. States were required to develop timelines through which they could measure and prove how and when their students would reach proficiency in several subjects. Schools were required to fill out annual "adequate yearly progress" reports in every subject—demonstrating, through metrics, if their school was functioning adequately, or if it should be labeled a "school in need of improvement."

The NCLB era became known as the time of "high-stakes testing" because of the extreme material consequences brought to bear on schools if students did not measure up on the rapidly proliferating forms of assessment. Poor ongoing results in any subject area were met with increasingly drastic sanctions. After five years of inadequate (and largely unattainable) progress, for example, a school was required to restructure, which meant a series of choices, all involving major changes to staffing, governance, and/or the form of the school itself. One of the choices was conversion to a charter school, and another was conversion to private management.[10] In many cases principals were replaced, often in favor of more reform-oriented candidates.

Administrative reorganization of this type was one of the many ramifications of NCLB. Some began to suspect that this was, in fact, one of the ultimate goals of the law. In addition to the waning interest in teacher input and shared governance, increasing hostility to teachers' unions became a notable feature of the new era.

Additionally, the strongly negative consequences of having students perform poorly on the annual standardized exams led to so-called "teaching to the test." Teachers desperately spent increasing amounts of time preparing students for taking the tests and devoted less time to discussion, critical analysis, creative classroom pursuits, and more social assessments of student learning and success. Their own skills in creating and refining curricula, devising methods of learning appropriate for their own students and classrooms, and producing systems of accountability that could encapsulate the entire learning experience were summarily brushed aside.[11]

Militarized Education and the War on Youth

The federal mandate to support low-performing students and schools was underfunded if funded at all during this period. Yet principals were at risk of school closure if student performance did not improve. Many critics have noted how this situation, where there were many sticks but few carrots, produced a culture of fear as the main motivator for actions to "reform." In the context of annual failing grades on the standardized forms of assessment, low morale for principals, teachers, parents, and students was compounded by the looming prospect of complete social dislocation and loss of jobs. It is not surprising that the reaction of many administrators was to "encourage" low-performing students to either stay away on the day tests were taken or to drop out of school altogether.[12]

Student dropout rates during this period increased for students of color and second-language learners.[13] Many researchers blamed this on both the high-stakes testing regime that encouraged schools to push students at the bottom out, as well as harsh zero-tolerance policies ushered in under Reagan and continued through Clinton and Bush. These policies made even small infractions, such as playground scuffles, grounds for suspension and in some cases expulsion. Henry Giroux, among others, has written about neoliberal policies in education as a "war" on youth, with the militarization of public high schools "so commonplace that even in the face of the most flagrant disregard for children's rights, such acts are justified by both administrators and the public on the grounds that they keep kids safe."[14]

The strict, high-stakes testing and zero-tolerance regimes affected students in poor, predominantly minority areas the most. While the era of zero tolerance has been ameliorated over the past decade, many of the other components of educational reform continued through the Obama presidency. Indeed, his Race to the Top (RttT) initiative was similarly oriented to entrepreneurialism, standardized testing and accountability measures, performance-based evaluations of teachers, and the expansion of charter schools, especially for the purpose of turning around "low-achieving" schools.[15] The initiative also continued public education's geographical shift away from local control and toward that of federal authorities. Moreover, RttT marked over three decades of federal educational policy—beginning with the Reagan administration—in which the goals of student preparation were more identifiably and concretely linked with labor market competitiveness rather than broader democratic aims.[16]

Not surprisingly, perhaps, the impoverished schools and neighborhoods of interest to the RttT designers were those most targeted for improvement by philanthropists. As noted earlier, philanthropic funding in the millennial moment manifests certain characteristics quite similar to the older era of Carnegie and Rockefeller, including the specific aim of connecting the disenfranchised and underprivileged to economic circuits through circumscribed and delimited forms of human capital development. During both periods, the larger, systemic problems of labor exploitation, social and economic inequality, and uneven development were obscured and left unaddressed.

Contemporary philanthropy, however, also reflects the flexible, short-term entrepreneurial strategies of contemporary capital accumulation processes. In education the money often flows not just to targeted schools in poor and minority neighborhoods, but also to cities with specific forms of governance in place—such as cities where there is mayoral control and the mayor is known to be supportive of large-scale educational reform. Mayoral control of school districts removes decision-making from elected school boards and silences the voices of those community members most affected by educational reform. Because it bypasses the time-consuming and often messy processes associated with democracy, it enables faster, top-down decision-making.

This form of political as well as geographical targeting indicates the desire for rapid, flexible, and measurable change. It is the type of educational transformation preferred by many private foundations, which can pull their money out of pilot reforms if they appear to be too strongly resisted and/or failing. These short-term, easy-exit reform projects can be scaled up, relocated, or ended with the same quick calculations and decision-making that helped make the fortunes of foundation CEOs.

Since schools are locally and culturally embedded and cannot be flexibly relocated or adapted in short time periods, pilot "failures" often produce profound bouts of chaos and destabilization for the affected schools and students. While possibly providing a learning instance for foundations, the quick exit from "non-performing" pilots adds to the problems besetting public institutions in the context of overall declining financial and moral support. This contributes to the narrative of the public school system as failing—the very same narrative that encouraged the reforms in the first place.

The Gates Foundation and Neoliberal Up-Scaling

There are many private foundations currently involved in education, but the Gates, Broad, and Walton foundations are the most prominent and, to date, most heavily invested in educational reform. In this section and the next I provide a few examples of the types of programs that were funded in Seattle and the overall leadership style, reform strategies, and personnel that were cultivated and promoted there by two of these foundations. The examples give a sense of how these actors have helped to shape policy as well as the shifting beliefs and values around public education and its role in producing workers and citizens.

The first example is from the Gates Foundation. Its small-schools initiative from 2000 to 2008 provides a good example of the piloting logic of contemporary philanthropic interventions in education. Convinced that small schools would provide a panacea for the ills of traditional high schools, the foundation invested $2 billion to break up larger comprehensive schools and establish smaller ones. Foundation money was given to schools and districts across the United States, impacting over 2,500 schools and almost 800,000 students. It was just as quickly withdrawn, however, when it appeared that the grants were not producing the desired results.

One of the most anticipated outcomes of the restructuring was a higher number of students going to college, part of the foundation's emphasis on "college-ready education." Various assessment measures seemed to indicate, however, that this was not happening—at least within the three-to-five year window during which most grant recipients were expected to demonstrate success. Over the course of eight years this lack of immediate, measurable attainment led to the early demise of the initiative and a redirection of foundation funding into other areas, most notably more advanced measures to assess teacher effectiveness, more standardized testing, and linking teacher pay with performance— as measured with quantitative forms of assessment.

In 2000, Seattle Public Schools (SPS) were among the first recipients of Gates Foundation money to implement the conversion of larger high schools into what were then termed small learning communities. It began with a $25.9 million renewable grant as part of a "model district initiative," with the money intended for all 97 schools in the district. A press release indicated that the grant was intended to increase access to technology as well as improve teaching and learning—part of a broader effort to "transform schools into twenty-first-century learning organizations in line with the Foundation's Attributes of High Achievement Schools."[17]

While some high schools welcomed the initiative, others resented the district's insistence on implementing a project that was clearly designed for underperforming schools. Local research in Seattle indicated that there was little interest in teacher buy-in during this time. Indeed, in many cases teachers were not even informed about the initiative. Additionally, administrators often felt overwhelmed by the increasing administrative complexity that accompanied the rapid creation of smaller schools out of the breakup of large high schools.

Even for those administrators and teachers who were enthusiastic at the beginning of the initiative, fatigue and resistance soon took over when they were confronted with the major changes and largely unfunded logistical challenges that had to be resolved in short order. Personnel turnover—a frequent occurrence with destabilizing and undemocratic reforms such as these—was also high, with the further result that some administrators' initial interest in the small learning communities transformation was lost through attrition as well.

Ultimately, many of the reforms mandated under the contracts did not occur. The foundation responded in 2005 with a refusal to renew the SPS grant. Thus after a mere five years and the dislocation of hundreds of students, teachers, and administrators, the Seattle initiative was ended, and schools were left to repair themselves as best they could. Many other schools and school districts across the United States experienced a similar traumatic withdrawal of foundation funds and severe dislocation during the same time period.[18]

One of the many criticisms of this disaster was the obvious disregard shown by the Gates Foundation and its staff to the school districts and personnel, as well as to education researchers. Despite Gates's strong pronouncements in support of evidence-based policy, the foundation paid scant attention to the data provided by education researchers, which was equivocal on the advantages of small specialist high schools versus larger comprehensive ones. While personalized instruction, closer mentoring, and more frequent interactions with teachers are clear benefits of smaller schools, because of the economies of scale larger comprehensive high schools are less expensive to operate. As a result, more resources in larger schools can be directed towards extra-curricular offerings, including sports and music programs, drama, and art. This advantage was not accorded as much weight as greater student–teacher interaction, however, as the latter is highly correlated with college readiness—a central goal of the Gates Foundation.

Further, there was little attention to the role of teachers in implementing the changes despite overwhelming research evidence that teacher buy-in is essential to the success of any educational reform. Finally, the fast tempo of the reforms, with a quick promotion of a preferred strategy, successful outcomes expected within a short time frame, and a rapid withdrawal of grant funding after the perceived failure, did not allow sufficient time for the changes to take hold. The perspective was the type one might expect in a corporate boardroom rather than a foundation operating on behalf of children. It indicated some of the impatience and hubris associated with contemporary philanthropy, where the expectation of financial and social returns is underpinned by a corporate mentality.

Additionally, there was a strong geographical impact of the pilot failure. A key, often unnoticed, effect of the small-schools debacle for SPS was a spatial and political shift in how grants were made. This shift indicated a broader restructuring of neoliberal practices involving PPPs. After the SPS "failure," rather than money being given directly to school districts, the Gates Foundation started lending to an intermediary organization called the Coalition for Essential Schools (CES). This organization soon became a central nodal point in the distribution of funding for small-school initiatives around the United States. CES now scrutinizes all grant recipients based on whether or not their values and commitments to reform line up with those of the foundation.

The establishment of the CES is consistent with a larger organizational shift to work above or outside the local level, with intermediaries that can be handpicked and are therefore more likely to do the exact bidding of the foundation. The key point here is that the Gates Foundation learned from its failed partnership with SPS. After it decided not to renew the district's grant, the foundation effectively rescaled its activities, moving away from intransigent local actors and complex bureaucracies to work directly with like-minded partners at the national scale.

Seeing local resistance and disinterest as a potential blockage to the realization of its educational reform priorities, the Gates Foundation altered its long-term strategy and its partnerships. The new direction reflected an entrenchment of neoliberal governmentality, in the sense of an increasing reliance on private-sector organizations and the wholesale circumventing of public-sector institutions and democratic forms of accountability. In the case of Seattle and many other nonconforming pilot recipients, when these community institutions and actors showed signs of resistance, fatigue, or even democratic disagreement, the educational reform bandwagon continued on without them and over them.

The Broad Foundation and the Corporatization of Leadership

My second illustration of philanthropic intervention in Seattle comes from the Eli and Edythe Broad Education Foundation. This foundation has been instrumental at multiple levels of educational reform but is perhaps best known for its leadership training programs, which include the Broad Center for the Management of School Systems and the Broad Institute for School Boards. The former is composed of two separate programs: the Broad Superintendents Academy and the Broad Residency in Urban Education. In *The Gift of Education*, Kenneth Saltman has documented the ways in which these programs seek to inculcate existing leadership practices in education with ideas and policies from the corporate world.[19]

The Broad Foundation's basic reform platform is underpinned with neoliberal ideas about the efficiency and superiority of the free market. The overarching premise of the foundation is that bad management and lack of choice are the twin ills that have beset poor schools and neighborhoods—not the havoc caused by free-market capitalism, patriarchy, and racism. It thus aims to "fix" these schools by bringing in private-sector assumptions about competition, choice, assessment, accountability, and better labor relations to the world of public education.

The logic of neoliberalism saturates the ideology and everyday practices of the foundation, from its push for leaders who advocate individual freedom and choice, to its attacks on those institutions that protect collective wages and rights. The ideology of individual responsibility is evident in the logic of consumer choice, as greater school choice gives parents the rights and the responsibility to choose well. It is also evident in the consistent push for standardized testing and accountability, as more tests enable greater benchmarking against others, which incites more competition, both between students and between schools.

In addition to numerous prizes and scholarships for individual and district "achievement"—as measured by standardized tests and in competition with others—the foundation also makes every effort to encourage the deregulation and privatization of teacher preparation programs and the expansion and entrenchment of charter schools. Through its actions it also undermines teacher autonomy and solidarity, and promotes the demise of teachers' unions. It does this with a multi-pronged strategy of leadership transformation at the scale of school boards, school principals, and school superintendents.

Much of the Broad Foundation's training promotes an authoritarian style of top-down leadership reminiscent of CEOs wielding their power in corporate boardrooms or generals on the battlefield. The reforms desired by the foundation are seen as strategic moves in a war of position, moves to take enemy lines that may be thwarted or slowed down by intransigent unions, uncooperative principals, or feisty parents. In order to win the battle, leaders adopt a take-no-prisoners form of governing—pushing changes hard and fast, regardless of the wishes of other education stakeholders, such as those of the community.

There is a clear disdain for democracy here as teachers and parents are shunted aside in the quest for rapid district-wide transformations. An authoritarian stance and rigid disciplinary action in the classroom also manifest a disregard for the basic rights of young people. Most distressingly, there is a distinctly racial component to this—once again reminiscent of the earlier targeted funding of the scientific philanthropy era.

Strong disciplinary methods in schools are most likely to occur in poor school neighborhoods and to be carried out on students of color. Specific minority populations are targeted through programs designed to address the so-called "achievement gap," a gap that these new, no-nonsense methods are expected to bridge. As Saltman notes:

> The turn to military leaders particularly for the urban poor and predominantly African American and Latino student bodies belies a profoundly racialized phenomenon within which these students are framed as suffering primarily from a lack of discipline, which the military and the corporation can supply.[20]

Principals and superintendents are thus brought in who are willing to run the school like a military training camp, with strict regimens, codes, uniforms, sanctions, and rote forms of obedience expected.

In a particularly disingenuous move, many of the superintendents trained by the Broad Foundation who are sent to turn around those students and districts perceived as ailing are themselves African-American. This is not a coincidence. It is part of the larger war of position, in which reform is pushed hard from above, while a tokenistic and manipulative push for consent is simultaneously sought from below.

Seattle provides a good example of this strategy. First led in the early reform years of the 1990s by an African-American retired army major general, John Stanford, the Seattle School Board later hired Maria Goodloe-Johnson, also African-American and a 2003 graduate of the Broad Superintendents Academy. Stanford had no background in education but was hailed for his "dynamic" leadership style—even before beginning in the position. Goodloe-Johnson had some experience and was also heavily touted as an agent of change.

One of Stanford's signature changes was to abandon race-based busing in 1996 in favor of magnet schools and greater school choice.[21] He was also a proponent of standardized testing, and further proposed student uniforms, sanctions against students allegedly involved with gangs, and allowing corporate sponsorship of afterschool and other extracurricular programs (although these latter proposals were not adopted because of opposition from parents). In his book *Victory in our Schools*, Stanford laid out his philosophy of district leadership: running schools like businesses.[22]

Despite his strong public advocacy of military and corporate styles of leadership, however, Stanford bowed to community pressure in many instances, and was perceived as a charismatic leader who cared deeply about the students. Further, his death after just three years in post occurred before much significant opposition to his style or proposed changes emerged and grew into a popular movement. The same could not be said of Goodloe-Johnson, who reigned as Seattle's school superintendent from 2007 to 2011 before she was fired by the Seattle School Board.

Goodloe-Johnson's leadership style and the many educational reforms she pushed through during her tenure were textbook examples of Broad Foundation training and ideology. Among the most insidious practices she learned and implemented from her training at the foundation's academy was the closure of existing schools rather than the attempt to improve or fix them. This was part of a broader strategy to produce overall changes to the system by fomenting chaos and disruption, or what came to be known in pro-reform circles as "churn." Reformers believe that churn is necessary in order to throw communities into turmoil, thus weakening their ability to oppose change.

In a very short period of time, Goodloe-Johnson was able to create an impressive amount of churn in the Seattle public school system. In implementing a new "capacity management plan" she closed five schools for a saving of $3.5 million, but then reopened five schools seven months later at a cost of $48 million. The closures in Seattle, especially the African American Academy, T.T. Minor and Cooper Elementary, disproportionately affected children of color and those with special needs. They also resulted in legal action against the district supported by the NAACP (National Association for the Advancement of Colored People).

In general this kind of turmoil and dislocation weakens communities and makes it easier for charter schools to gain a foothold, especially in minority neighborhoods.

Goodloe-Johnson also created churn through repeated attacks on teachers, including laying off teachers during "teacher appreciation week" and then rehiring many of the same personnel a short time later. Her toxic relationship with teachers was compounded by her promotion of Teach for America, a program touted by reformers that allows recent college graduates without a Masters degree in education to compete with those who have been credentialed through university training programs. In addition to closing schools and acting in bad faith on teachers' contract negotiations, Goodloe-Johnson mandated increased high-stakes testing for students, and tied teacher evaluations to student performance on these tests.

Overall, the reforms pushed by Goodloe-Johnson in Seattle are illustrative of the larger changes sought by the Broad Foundation and by many of the other philanthropists involved in education. They combine an authoritarian, undemocratic leadership style with transformations that undermine social systems of community and solidarity. Instead, they celebrate market-based ideologies of individualism, competition, and choice. This is part of a broader transformation in capitalism involving new kinds of PPPs. Altogether, the new partnerships and programs manifest sweeping changes in the structure of education and in the ways that people think about what it should do and be.

Despite these changes, however, there are also a number of similarities with philanthropic interventions in the past. Among these, the most glaring is the ongoing targeting of communities of color for educational reform. Whether the discourse is youth "at risk" or closing the "achievement gap," the ultimate goal and many of the methods are the same. These include discipline and regimentation, with the ultimate aim of creating productive workers for a flexible economy. In the next chapter I examine some of the ways that these processes also lead towards another goal of reformers: the privatization of education.

7
The Choice Machine and the Road to Privatization

In this chapter I look at how people involved in education are recruited as entrepreneurial, choice-making subjects and how this is implicated in the longer-term transition towards the privatization of education. My focus is on the popular media and on the various "expert" reports and statistics that are funded by private foundations to encourage parents to advocate for reforms.

As discussed in earlier chapters, educational stakeholders are enlisted by public–private partnerships (PPPs) through the refrain of public school failure. Moreover, not only are they recruited into these market-mediated resolutions, they are simultaneously directed away from making demands of the state for money or support. It is important to analyze this personal reorientation because it shows how attention can be shifted from horizontal forms of provision—such as government-funded systems—to more market-mediated ones—such as charter schools, vouchers, and learning academies. It involves both a structural reorientation towards the quasi or full privatization of education, and the simultaneous cultivation and enlistment of individuals as choice-making subjects.

The idea of "choice" and its articulation with freedom is one of the critical liberal rationalities underpinning market systems. Milton Friedman argued that providing parents with vouchers so that they could choose the schools their children attended was the only solution "to break the monopoly, introduce competition and give the customers alternatives."[1] For Friedman, and many contemporary educational reformers, state-funded schools were monopolistic suppliers, socialistic enterprises that should be broken up and privatized so that parents—as consumers—could exert their influence through choice, thus forcing schools to improve through the forces of competition.

In countries such as the United States, the United Kingdom, and Canada, where public education has been considered a human right and a public good for well over a century, however, the notion of educational privatization does not seem as natural or obvious as it was to Friedman and other neoliberal economists. Thus for contemporary actors, who are similarly interested in creating similar beliefs about the essential rationality and efficiency of private education systems, it is necessary to encourage and promote these types of ideas. Moreover, the existing system has to be shaken up—through narratives of school failure and through the forces of "churn," as documented in the previous chapter.

Yet these strategies of inducing agreement and consent for school privatization and greater choice are only possible if educational alternatives are provided. Further, parents have to know how to choose once they are no longer obligated to attend their local school and, in theory at least, have a wider range of schools from which to select. In education, the technologies of neoliberal governance encourage parental responsibility for making the correct choices in the context of expert knowledge. The assumption of philanthropists and politicians is that if the appropriate expertise is provided for measuring and assessing teachers and schools, then parents will be nudged not just to make the right school choices for their children, but also to become believers in choice and in neoliberal reforms more generally.

Thus the neoliberal rationalities of education reform are such that the technologies of expertise—in the form of standardized tests, consultants' reports, and other metrics of expert evaluation—are provided and encouraged, along with the appropriate cultural and financial incentives. With this expertise, persuasion, and support from above, the expectation is that parents and other actors, such as school boards, administrators, principals and teachers, will make the appropriate prudential calculations and pursue the most rational choice of action for their children, schools, and districts.

In the United States, in addition to providing funding that seeks to open up the field of choice, such as to charter schools, charter management organizations, politicians supportive of charters and vouchers, and non-professional teaching corps programs such as Teach for America, grants are also directed towards institutions that provide educational "expertise." These include education reform advocacy organizations, think tanks, research centers, consultants, and standardized testing corporations and accreditation boards. Grants are also conferred on the most direct consumers of education: parent groups. Additionally, in a number of instances, foundation funding has subsidized various forms of cultural persuasion, including advertising, as well as popular documentaries and movies that promote the advantages of greater parental choice. Often this funding converges in a frenzy of activity around supposed parent activism that can be documented and disseminated in the media and through popular cultural events.

Promoting Choice through Media and Politics

Most foundations interested in educational reform supply some form of seed funding to parent groups that agitate for greater school choice. These groups are represented in the popular media and on foundation websites as parents who have become infuriated with their low-quality neighborhood schools and have spontaneously organized to demand more choice for their children. Many of the parents represented in this domain are African-American or Hispanic.

A recent example of this type of representation in popular culture is the 2012 Hollywood movie *Won't Back Down*, in which two mothers take on apathetic teachers and a sclerotic teachers' union to try to turn around their children's failing school.[2] According to the promotional blurb for the movie, "this powerful story of parenthood, friendship and courage mirrors events that are making headlines daily." The setting for the film is a down-and-out postindustrial blue-collar neighborhood of Pittsburgh, Pennsylvania, and the main cast is a mix of working-class whites and African-Americans who rise to the seemingly insurmountable challenge of taking over and renewing the dreadful school.

Won't Back Down was co-produced by Walden Media, also a key player in the financing and distribution of the highly popular 2010 documentary *Waiting for "Superman"* (additionally financed by the Gates and Broad foundations).[3] Walden Media is owned by the Anschutz Family Foundation, a major donor to conservative US think tanks, including the Manhattan Institute, Cato Institute, and Heritage Foundation. All three of these think tanks are heavily influenced by the writings of von Hayek and Friedman and are strong promoters of school choice and educational privatization.

The focus of *Waiting for "Superman"* is on the failure of inner-city state schools, with poor children of color and their parents among the main protagonists. Both the movie and the documentary focus on the power and importance of parental activism in demanding better schools and teachers for their children. Parents are shown as initially frustrated and helpless in the face of intransigent bureaucracies and the bad quality education their children are receiving. However, by the end of both films, the fictitious mothers of *Won't Back Down* and many of the real mothers and fathers in *Waiting for "Superman"* are depicted as energized parent activists.

Research into many of these "parent" organizations, however, indicates that they were either initially established or are currently managed by individuals working for charter school reforms or who are otherwise connected to the broader world of foundation-financed education reform. This was the case for the organization Parent Revolution, which promoted the spread of parent trigger laws across the United States. Parent trigger laws allow parents to take over and transform "failing" state schools—the type of "trigger" process employed by the mothers in *Won't Back Down*. After a takeover, parents can fire the existing staff and/ or turn the school over to a private charter management organization.

Parent Revolution was established by Ben Austin, a former policy consultant for the charter school organization Green Dot. Both Green Dot and Parent Revolution were provided funding by the Gates, Walton, and Broad foundations.[4] Several other ostensibly parent-run or grassroots organizations have similar histories of charter involvement and big philanthropy connections. In addition to Parent Revolution these include education reform advocacy organizations such as the League of Education Voters, StudentsFirst, Stand for Children, Democrats for Education Reform, and Better Education for Kids among others.[5]

A recent example of these multilayered interconnections can be seen in the funding and promotion of charter schools. For example, in the documentary *Waiting for "Superman"*, pro-reformer Bill Gates is interviewed, along with the pro-reform superintendent of the Washington, DC school system, Michelle Rhee. They each make statements lambasting the poor quality of public education. Rhee makes many disparaging comments about teachers and teachers' unions, and Gates expounds further on the importance of education for the global economy. At the end of the documentary parents are shown waiting for the results of five charter school lotteries, including the Harlem Success Academy.

All of these parents desperately want access to a charter school, which is presented as vastly superior to their local state-funded school. The message of the documentary is unequivocal: this lottery "choice" will determine whether or not these urban, predominantly minority children will be able to obtain a decent education and be brought into the world of economic connection and employment.

One of the most insidious aspects of the documentary—produced at the height of the global recession and amidst high unemployment in every sector of the US economy—was the implication that this crisis was due primarily to the nation's uneducated workforce, rather than the criminal mismanagement of the financial sector. Bill Gates, for example, reports in the interview that there are not enough educated workers for the high-tech economy. The director and narrator, Davis Guggenheim, then propounds that companies (such as Microsoft, presumably) thus have to hire from outside the United States. The documentary suggests that by 2020 there will be just 50 million workers with the educational requirements necessary for a presumed 120 million high-tech job openings. Despite ongoing examples of racism in hiring practices as well as the oversupply of college graduates and spatial reorganization of work discussed in Part I, the implication is that if only students were better educated in charter schools they would be able to avail themselves of these shiny new high-tech employment opportunities.

Some of the behind-the-scenes processes not shown in the documentary include a campaign called Flooding the Zone, which was initiated and promoted by the Success Charter Network and Democrats for Education Reform (DFER). This campaign was initiated with the explicit purpose of creating greater parental support in Harlem for opening more charter schools. DFER coordinated the rally and the Success Charter Network spent $1.3 million on leaflets, mailings, ads, posters, and paid canvassing of the Harlem neighborhood between 2007 and 2009, just prior to and during the same period in which the documentary was being made.[6] These two organizations received funding from several private philanthropy organizations, including the Gates, Walton, and Broad foundations.

What is also not shown in the documentary is the connection between the pro-charter school organizations working in Harlem and hedge funds. Many of the members of the board of directors of DFER were hedge fund managers. The board of trustees for the Harlem Children's Zone and Success Charter Network were similarly populated with financial and hedge fund managers.[7] Indeed, a strong, ongoing connection between hedge funds, the promotion of charter schools, and attacks on teachers' unions has been documented by a number of sources, who also note the links of these members of the financial elite to think tanks, politicians, and economic actions profoundly damaging to the populations the charters claim to serve.[8]

The steering and funding of parents and parent groups illustrated here parallels the promotion and support of politicians who push educational reform. This includes governors and mayors eager to take control of schools from elected school boards. A recent study by Sarah Reckhow confirmed that the networking between and shared goals of foundations advocating educational reform leads them to target specific schools and school districts.[9] These targeted sites are located in districts with mayoral or governor control, thus providing a greater chance for leveraging educational reform through long-term policy change. By concentrating their funding on these politicians and locations, foundations attempt to achieve greater influence in these places.

Overall, the intersections discussed here show the reform coalition in action: a set of alliances comprising venture capitalists, philanthropists, and politicians bent on dismantling state-funded education and opening up the terrain to private interests. These alliances are geographically aware and sensitive, targeting specific neighborhoods and populations to serve as the preliminary nodes in the construction of a broader privatization network.

These partnerships, which are almost invariably hidden from public view, use the tactics of consent—attempting to recruit parents through popular culture and other social media. They acknowledge the despair of parents whose children attend poor-quality schools. Rather than lay the responsibility for these unsupported schools in financially deprived neighborhoods and inequitable systems of resource allocation where it belongs, the alliances point parents towards charters and other market-mediated systems for remediation and the hope of future redemption. The high hopes and promises of these schools are uneven, however, with some performing better than the neighborhood school but many performing worse. Moreover, for those that do succeed, a frequent cost is to the local (non-charter) school, which is left with those children and parents unable to access the charter school for a variety of reasons, discussed further in following sections.[10]

Inculcating Choice through Expert Knowledge

Another area in which philanthropy foundations are heavily invested is education research. Foundations conduct or commission research on topics involving charter schools, standardized tests, teacher-performance assessments, and other issues connected with education reform. The research is generally commissioned by non-profit organizations and almost invariably employs quantitative methods. The use of metrics enables foundations to frame findings as "evidence-based," as opposed to the experience of teachers or democratic discussions in public forums, which are denigrated as anecdotal or beholden to special interests such as unions.

Often these research units are located in think tanks and universities, which bring an even more enhanced aura of objectivity to the research's results. A good example is the Center for Reinventing Public Education (CRPE) at the University of Washington, Bothell. This unit has been supported by both private-sector grants provided by the Gates Foundation, along with several other reform-minded organizations, including the Carnegie, Dell, and Walton foundations, and public-sector grants and resources from the US Department of Education and the university.

CRPE, which employs 13 white self-proclaimed "experts" and 17 white affiliates on its research team, emphasizes its objectivity and neutrality, despite its mission dedicated to education reform. Among the CRPE's core beliefs, as stated on their website, is the necessity for state-funded schools to have greater "freedom" to innovate while also being held "accountable" to equity and high performance. They "formulate new ideas for governance structures (including changing roles for local school boards, state education agencies, and the federal government) and ways to improve accountability measures." Even more pointedly they ask, "How can civic leaders create a school choice system that works for all families?"[11]

Despite their own clear mandate on behalf of greater school choice, the research that is produced is framed as evidence-based, both in CRPE's statements and in reiterations by those employing the data on behalf of choice-related policies and laws. California Congressman George Miller, senior Democrat of the House Education and Workforce Committee wrote, for example:

CRPE first grabbed my attention with its work on school finance and equity, and I have continued to rely on its expertise as I have crafted education policy in Congress. CRPE's balanced, evidence-based, and forward-thinking approach to improving our education system has been invaluable. In all of its work, CRPE boldly takes on the status quo and focuses on what is in the best interest of students.[12]

The results of this "balanced" and "evidence-based" research almost invariably demonstrates the success of "forward-thinking" reform projects or else strong indicators of the necessity and advantages of initiating education reform. Charter schools in particular are favored by the analysts, even though people may be against them. For example, Washington state residents voted thrice (in 1996, 2000, and 2004) against allowing charters in their state. This was before large amounts of money from several foundations and private individuals, including Bill Gates, Eli Broad, Sam Walton, Paul Allen, and Jeff Bezos, were given to the pro-charter campaign and effected a slim electoral victory for charter schools at the polls in 2012. (The initiative had a fundraising advantage of 50 to 1.) This decision was later blocked by the Washington Supreme Court in 2015, but then reinstated in a new form, with Bill Gates partially bankrolling existing charter schools.[13]

Policy reports, op-eds, journal articles, and other writings on the advantages of charter schools are the most prominent among the CRPE's prolific research output. Most of these are premised on ways to improve school-choice implementation through providing "evidence-based" solutions to the multiple problems that have been linked with educational reform. CRPE introduces some of the difficulties and problems associated with charter schools. These include low enrollments of low-performing students, high suspension rates, re-segregation, and enrollment gaps between traditional schools and charters vis-à-vis the education of English language learners and students with special educational needs. Then it offers proposals for ways to fix or counteract these problems.

This liberal nostrum is one in which the underlying values of freedom, choice, opportunity, and inclusion are vaunted as the desired and expected norm. If they are failing in practice, it is only as a result of poor implementation or bad management. The underpinning violence and dispossession of the neoliberalizing reform system as a whole, and charter schools in particular, is unseen, unheard, and undisclosed.

The story of these policy centers working in affiliation with universities is linked with the broader narrative of PPPs that have expanded with philanthropic funding over the past two decades. Public institutions are able to project an image of neutrality that corporations find difficult to maintain. Thus these institutions and those working in them are cultivated and encouraged into alliances and partnerships through grants, publicity, and prestige. As one former Seattle teacher noted vis-à-vis applying for a Gates grant in 2011, "everybody is getting money from the Gates Foundation."[14] Policy debates are greatly influenced by the research reports and pronouncements of these hybrid institutes and groups, which appear on the surface to be unbiased public-sector entities, but which are beholden to vast amounts of private foundation funding for their very survival.

Investigating these types of alliances, the types of neutral expertise they project, and the forms of choice they try to inculcate is critical because they are forming the pathways and leading the charge towards the privatization of education. While these processes have received fresh support in the United States from the Trump administration and the pro-reform Education Secretary, Betsy DeVos, the privatization of state-funded schooling has been on the conservative agenda for quite some time. Conservative think tanks such as the American Enterprise Institute, the Cato Institute, the Manhattan Institute, the Hoover Institution, and the Heritage Foundation, among others, have devoted a considerable amount of attention to education over the past several decades.

Drawing on the ideology of Milton Friedman and buoyed by Reagan's 50-percent cut to federal funding for schools in low-income school districts—alongside his (failed) attempts to push voucher legislation through Congress—these right-wing think tanks began a concerted advance to liberalize education in the early 1980s. As vouchers were not yet acceptable to the public or legislators, philanthropists and corporate think tanks began to back the charter school movement as an intermediary step along the pathway to privatization.

Estimates of the vast amounts of money to be reaped by the corporate world with the charter movement and the eventual privatization of education are in the tens of billions. Indeed, the massive transfer of funds from the public to the private sector is already well on its way. The US Department of Education has funneled hundreds of millions of dollars to education alliances and other types of PPPs subcontracted by the state over the past two decades alone. These include policy centers, private accrediting agencies for teacher training, institutions developing new textbooks and accountability techniques for the now mandated standardized tests, and charter schools, among others.[15]

Charters and charter management organizations have become big business, buoyed by donations from philanthropists alongside public-sector handouts of space, resources, and money. For-profit charters often show the poorest results with respect to graduation rates and test scores, but they remain open and profitable because of low costs. Costs are kept low through their business strategy of risk management: "keeping the winners and discarding the losers."[16] Children, that is.

Charters have caused the deracination of public education in several cities, including New Orleans, Detroit, Washington, Flint, and Cleveland. In addition to the damage caused to the state school system, a significant "side effect" of the introduction of charters is a growing racial and economic re-segregation of the school population.[17] Other negative outcomes for charter schools indicated in many studies include higher rates of expulsion and a significantly lower enrollment of English-language learners and students with disabilities.

The corporate takeover of schools is similar in many ways to the privatization of prisons and the formation of the prison–industrial complex in the United States. Privatization enables corporations to enrich themselves through public sector payouts and access to public resources while at the same time damaging those it has committed to serve. This is perhaps most evident in the closure of state schools and the subsequent harm inflicted on entire communities, mostly African-American and poor.

School Closures and Urban Dispossession

Over the past decade many parents in low-income and segregated neighborhoods in the United States have experienced the closure of "failing" local schools, often instigated by pro-reform mayors and school superintendents. Reform-minded foundations and politicians believe that parents should become savvy investors for their children, choosing the best school environments that lead to the strongest individual returns. But for many parents in poor neighborhoods these "choices" disappear with the closure of their neighborhood school, as does their sense of community and often their very economic survival.

Significant numbers of school closures have occurred in Philadelphia, Chicago, Detroit, Newark, and Oakland since 2013. In that year alone, Philadelphia closed 23 schools and Chicago closed 49—the largest number in US history. In both cases there was massive community opposition to the closures, but it went unheeded. And in both cases African-Americans were the hardest hit. In Chicago, African-Americans composed 88 percent of the residents affected by the closures, even though they made up just 40 percent of the school-district population at the time; in Philadelphia the figure was 81 percent.[18]

School closures have many effects, including destabilizing communities, the loss of unionized jobs (with African-American teachers the primary sufferers), and sometimes empty buildings that can become magnets for vandalism and crime. The rationale for closures is cost savings, and affected communities are enticed with the prospect of better schools in more efficient and up-to-date buildings. In fact the reverse is often the case. Not only do students frequently end up with inexperienced teachers in even more segregated and often lower functioning charter schools (as in New Orleans and Chicago), but their neighborhoods themselves become the targets of predatory forms of speculative capitalism.

This occurs through a number of processes, the primary one being what David Harvey termed accumulation by dispossession.[19] As schools are closed and the land or buildings sold, public assets belonging to the community are lost. At the same time, the chance for profit from these assets is turned over to the private developers who purchased them. Thus as the community is dispossessed of its commonly held assets, the potential for capital accumulation is gained by private owners.

This contemporary process can be linked to the older concept of primitive accumulation, famously identified by Marx as one of the key galvanizing forces of early capitalism. Marx noted the necessity of privatizing the means of production, such as commonly held land, so that the newly created landless proletariat would be forced to work as "free" wage laborers in the growing factories and other industrial activities of the era. This is because in order for the capitalist to be able to purchase labor power effectively, the laborer must have been separated from their own means of production and have no effective means of survival other than through the sale of their labor power. "Money can be expended in this form only because labour-power finds itself in a state of separation from its means of production."[20] At the same time, the land that was seized could be sold as a private good, thus augmenting the generation of capital.

Accumulation by dispossession is the recent iteration of primitive accumulation, occurring as a result of the neoliberal policies of privatization and financialization initiated in the 1970s and that gained ground over the following decades. Often those who were and remain first and most easily dispossessed are the indigenous, minorities, and the poor, as they generally have fewer resources and less cultural capital with which to fight the theft. In the case of closed schools in African-American urban neighborhoods this was clearly the case.

Additionally, the closure and privatization of schools can have the further (often intended) impact of accelerating the processes of financial speculation and gentrification. In Philadelphia, for example, the Edward Bok Technical High School, valued at $17.8 million, was sold by the city for $2.1 million to a developer who quickly turned the school into a "new and innovative center for Philadelphia creatives and non-profits."[21] The new center has recently launched a rooftop bar, attracting the young and hip to an area already beset by rising prices and the incipient forces of urban renewal and minority displacement.

In *The New Political Economy of Urban Education*, Pauline Lipman renders explicit the geographical connections between the education reform agenda, the privatization of public resources, and neoliberal urban restructuring.[22] In particular, she shows how, in city after city, school closure is integral to plans by the urban elite to create mega-developments in newly vacated spaces. Chicago's Renaissance 2010 plan, for example, targeted the African-American neighborhood of Bronzeville for real estate development, beginning with the demolition of thousands of public housing units and 70 neighborhood schools. One of the consequences of the development, including the demoralization of communities deprived of the schools that often served as important sources of history and connection, was the immediate gentrification of the area—which was part of the overall agenda. An additional aspect of the Renaissance plan was the opening of 100 charter schools.

The connection between these processes and the financial meltdown of 2008 is important to note here as well. Subprime mortgages during the Great Recession were widespread and affected homeowners across the United States. But in many urban neighborhoods they were also part of a deliberate predatory effort to strip equity from black homeowners.[23] School closures can be seen in this context as the secondary wave of accumulation by dispossession that systematically targets poor urban populations. Equity was stripped from the homes of African-Americans in the first wave, then from the schools of minority communities in the second.

This ongoing sordid process is part of the much longer history of racial capitalism, where flows of capital are linked to the formation and exploitation of black and brown subjects worldwide. As Watkins showed in his study of white philanthropy interventions in African-American education and life, this occurred historically through forces of coercion such as incarceration, induction in the military, and lynching, but also ideologically through the production of consent, via the church, and forms of philanthropic investment and aid.[24]

In the contemporary era, coercion and consent often fuse in the notion of choice—something that is increasingly necessary to make. In a sense this takes Marx's famous aphorism about history from *The Eighteenth Brumaire* one step further. Under conditions of neoliberal globalization, people make choices, but not under conditions of their own choosing. Moreover, when it comes time to make the necessary choice, it is discovered that there is only one choice to make.

Choice, Learning Academies, and Privatization in the United Kingdom

In the United Kingdom, the expansion of parental choice has also been an important part of the political agenda regarding educational policy since the late 1980s. This is the case despite changes in the parties in government: from Conservative to Labour, to Conservative–Liberal Democrat coalition, and back to Conservative again. The rationale is a neoliberal one. It is assumed that by giving parents the freedom to choose where their child is enrolled—and by diversifying the menu of options available—schools will increase their performance in the face of competition from other institutions. Attempts to increase parental choice have, as a result, gone hand in hand with attempts to marketize and managerialize a state-funded system of education, and to open it up more fully to the flows of capital and to additional modes of governance.

The 1988 Education Reform Act is an early example of how the expansion of choice in education was yoked to the language of free-market efficiencies and better management. With the Education Reform Act in place, parents were given the right to express their preference among the six schools their child could attend. This choice was expanded alongside the more general marketization of the education system. Because financing remained public but independent providers were allowed to compete for contracts, the Education Reform Act marked one of the first attempts to establish a "quasi market" within England's education sector.[25]

The Education Reform Act further diminished the governing role of local institutions by allowing schools to bypass the local scale and receive most of their budget directly from government. It also required school performance to be published in so-called league tables or rankings and the establishment of a national assessment framework, encouraging competition and providing templates for comparing and choosing between institutions.

The 1988 act was significant in another way for allowing City Technology Colleges (CTCs), first introduced by the Conservative government in 1986, to serve as a pilot network.[26] With a curriculum emphasizing technology and business, CTCs were intended to improve education quality in urban centers by combining public funding with private entrepreneurialism. The goal of these PPPs was to attract financial support and business sponsors to help fund infrastructural development, while at the same time encouraging students to attend by offering an innovative, business-oriented curriculum.[27]

While eventually deemed a failure, CTCs are noteworthy for their experimental organizational form. They were owned (or leased) and run by private-sector sponsors. The funding continued to come largely from government sources, but it was allotted in seven-year contracts and bypassed local governance structures. The funding structure, which facilitated greater autonomy for individual schools at the cost of control by local authorities, was in stark contrast to how state-funded education in England was traditionally managed at the time.

The CTC pilot network, along with charter schools in the United States, provided an early model for the Academies program that was initiated in 2000 by the New Labour government.[28] Similar to the charter school rhetoric, the purported aim of the program was to address inequalities in education, with a specific focus on "inner city children."[29] The term "inner city children" was a clear signifier that the schools were conceived, at least initially, to benefit poor, primarily immigrant and minority families.

At first, such institutions were restricted to secondary schools, although now some primary schools are academies. Similar to CTCs, academies receive funding directly from central government and thus exist outside the control of local education authorities. They are officially defined as "all-ability, state-funded schools established and managed by sponsors from a wide range of backgrounds, including high-performing schools and colleges, universities, individual philanthropists, businesses, the voluntary sector and the faith communities."[30] For a given academy, the sponsors set up a non-profit academy trust (a private company with charity status) for the purposes of governance and strategic oversight. These trusts, which are often part of larger academy chains, maintain legal but not financial accountability, the burden of which falls mostly on the state (although sponsors contribute around 20 percent of capital costs).[31]

Originally, the New Labour government established a target goal of 400 academies, with 200 slated to open by 2010. These figures increased dramatically, especially after the coalition government assumed power and passed the Academies Act 2010, enabling schools to convert to academies and for new academies, called "free schools," to be founded.[32] There are no restrictions on who can establish a free school, nor is there a requirement to involve parents, the local authority, or local community.[33]

As of 2016, out of 3,381 secondary schools (ages 11 to 18) in England, 2,075 are now academies. Academies are gaining ground at the primary school level as well, with 2,440 of 16,766 schools achieving academy status. Furthermore, then-chancellor George Osborne announced in May 2016 that all schools must convert to academies by 2020 or commit to converting by 2022.[34]

Since academies were first introduced, studies have found no evidence indicating that they produce better results in student performance than the local authority schools they replace.[35] In fact, recent data suggests just the opposite. In 2016, the first league table comparing local authority and multi-academy trusts (MATs) showed that academy chains constituted the lowest performing primary and secondary schools. In addition, there were more local-authority-controlled schools in the highest performing school group than academy chains.[36]

Academies are not required to follow the national curriculum. Sponsors must offer a curriculum that is "broad and balanced," but they are given significant leeway in interpreting exactly what that means. They can choose to highlight a particular area of emphasis, termed a "specialism," which can serve as a way to market the school to parents. Parents can thus be recruited through appeals to a specialized set of interests, one that purports to be the best "fit" for the child.

This has raised much public scrutiny, especially at the beginning of the academies programs when religious sponsors, such as the Vardy

Foundation, imported creationism into their schools.[37] Studies have also found that business values were being grafted onto, and normalized within, academy curricula such that "academies are predominantly being constructed as sites intended to enhance the growing influence of private versions of entrepreneurialism."[38]

Another area of debate involving academies is that of student selectivity. Academy trusts determine their school's admissions criteria. Although these must meet the national admissions codes, issues have been raised about preference given to certain students over others. There is growing evidence that the specialized admissions criteria of academies and free schools, regardless of their intentions, exclude children from poorer families.[39] Because of the pressure to succeed in the educational marketplace, school administrators feel pressure to weed out "risky" students—often those from disadvantaged backgrounds who are more likely to struggle in the classroom.

As academies become the norm, and as business knowledge and market competition become core elements of education, institutional and individual "success" become defined by what produces surplus value. Value, in this case, concerns the improvement of individual life chances and the creation of advantage over others. The creation of surplus value in schooling thus begins to depend more and more on competitive processes that create winners and losers among children. Moreover, this process often reproduces existing inequities and forms of social stratification. The original purported goal of academies—to raise the educational standards of underachieving areas—becomes self-defeating when achievement is defined according to the very processes that created social hierarchies in the first place.

As with charter schools in the United States, despite the initial rhetoric of equity and opportunity, success for the entrepreneurial academy has become bound to practices of social segregation and the reproduction of poverty. Indeed, recent empirical studies of academies have found that academies, regardless of their original purposes, do not reduce segregation nor do they increase social equity in education.[40] I would argue further that academies actually reinforce segregation—to the extent that such schools naturalize flows of capital. Not only do academies normalize business values such as entrepreneurialism, but they also present potential sites for surplus-value creation. Although legally considered not-for-profit, academy trusts may outsource work to private companies. As academy chains grow, and individual corporate sponsors control a larger number of schools, there is concern that sponsors will be in a position to profit from the outsourcing of auxiliary services, construction, and infrastructural support.

Recently, for example, the Bright Tribe Multi-Academy Trust came under fire for their contracting practices. Bright Tribe was established by Mike Dwan, a venture capitalist with plans to run over 200 academies. It became apparent that Bright Tribe was outsourcing facilities management to one of Dwan's own business interests. In this case the public educational sector served as a sinkhole for capital investment, a way to reap new returns from government coffers. As the *Guardian* put it, the "story of Mike Dwan is the story of an English state education system that has been thrown open to private business interests in unprecedented fashion."[41] If academies increase the autonomy of schools in managing themselves, and of parents in choosing where their children are enrolled, then they also increase the autonomy of capital within everyday life.

Public–Private Partnerships and the Commoditization of Education

In this part of the book I have examined the coalition of new actors and institutions currently involved in education reform. Philanthropy foundations are the most important of these new institutions, forming partnerships with governments as well as for-profit and not-for-profit organizations. The rise of PPPs between all of these players is the key story of the new millennium, affecting many areas of development, but with particularly strong ramifications in health and education.

One of the most important corollaries to this shift away from horizontal systems of provision is the movement toward the privatization of education. This is especially prominent in the United States, but can also be seen in the rise of learning academies in England and in emerging education policies in some Canadian provinces.[42] As part of broader efforts to inculcate positive ideas about privatizing education, many private foundations have funded the media, universities, and other institutions to help promote the purported efficiencies of market-based forms of choice. In this chapter I examined a few of these organizations, including popular movies and documentaries as well as university research centers.

In many cases the worst effects of increased marketization in education are felt in poor neighborhoods. This is owing to the dispossession and privatization of public resources—such as schools—that generally benefits private developers rather than the surrounding community. Further, these processes are often part of larger redevelopment projects that spur gentrification and residential dislocation.

In the next section of the book I look at some of the ways that residents of these communities fight back against these forces, rejecting the commoditization of education and claiming their schools and neighborhoods for themselves. A key aspect of this spatial struggle, I argue, is a knowledge of history as well as of geography. In the next chapter I give some examples of these ongoing battles for social justice, highlighting in particular the important role of educating students in radical geographies of community, both past and present.

PART IV

Geographies of Resistance, Acts of Citizenship

8
Taking Back Our Schools and Cities

The reform coalition is powerful, well-connected and wealthy, but it is not invincible. Resistance to school privatization and to the rhetoric of failure and choice is growing daily, with examples in multiple cities across the United States. In the United Kingdom and Canada there are similar voices opposed to the insidious encroachment of the market into the educational sphere.

Parents, students, teachers, and administrators write, march, and organize to protest against school closures, high-stakes testing, attacks on teachers, the push for charter schools and academies, and declining resources for the public school system. These are citizenship acts, democratic practices that define and reconfigure not only the cause but also those who are acting. Thus while the coalition to reform schools has had early successes in promoting a neoliberal agenda in education, it has also engendered a growing awareness and politicization of many individuals and groups opposed to it.

Changes to the environment in which people live, attend school, and go to work are immediate and visceral. They instigate and galvanize them to action, and in this process they are formed and reformed as political actors and subjects. In this sense, the production of space is deeply intertwined with the formation of political subjectivities in a mutually constitutive process.

Before continuing on with some examples of these resistant and disruptive subjects, it is useful to take one step back to consider key theoretical frameworks in which subjectivity formation has been analyzed. Because it ties directly into the discussion of the spatial politics and agency of these struggles, I will highlight some of the work of geographers in this area.

Althusser was one of the earliest theorists to link ideological production and the formation of subjectivity. He examined many of the major social institutions in society, including education, arguing that these ideological apparatuses aided in the reproduction of the conditions of production, and thus the ability of capitalism to continue despite its inherent contradictions. He was concerned especially with the reproduction of wage labor, and the ways that "non-repressive" or ideological mechanisms (education, religion, law, the family, and so on) produced working subjects within the capitalist system.[1]

Althusser's ideas were part of a broader corpus of work in Marxist theory analyzing the relationship between production, framed as the "base" of the capitalist system, and social reproduction, considered to be the "superstructure." His work was innovative at the time because of its emphasis on the relative autonomy of ideological apparatuses, that is, the ways that institutions such as education are structured within relations of dominance yet also maintain their own internal dynamics.

Nevertheless, the ways that Althusser theorized from above, abstracting away from concrete material relations and spaces, led him to miss certain fundamental aspects of these institutions, and thus the broader relationship between production and social reproduction. Most of social reproduction in the United States, and indeed throughout recorded history—that is, the work considered to be "outside" of production, either unwaged or paid so poorly it cannot serve to reproduce the laborer himself or herself—has been conducted by slaves and their descendants, immigrants, and women. This fundamental and seemingly obvious positionality, vis-à-vis who it is that engages in what kinds of labor, was elided in Althusser's analysis. In order to really understand how labor power is constituted as a class, and capitalism is reproduced as an economic system, we must understand how these particular groups are constituted as workers (waged and unwaged) within this system.[2]

In terms of institutions such as education and how they help to uphold and maintain inequitable relations of production, it is imperative to investigate the particular ideologies at work. How, for example, are African-American parents recruited (or "interpellated" in Althusser's terms) as "good parents" if they opt for school choice and send their children to charter schools? Elucidating how people come to have certain feelings about education and make certain decisions about schooling requires a nuanced understanding of both the coercive and the non-repressive disciplining processes that influence the formation of individual and group subjectivities.

The first step in this process is to investigate the ways in which individual, group, and societal understandings of schools, work, and value are ideologically produced in specific, material conditions and practices. Individuals are constituted as thinking, feeling, acting subjects in specific places, with identities formed both through the material conditions of those spaces and also through their performances and practices within them. Geographers emphasize the grounded, material nature of this as the "spatial imperative of subjectivity."[3]

Subjectivity is a product and process of practices that are constrained by normative assumptions about, for example, gender, sexuality, and race— and the kinds of sites and spaces that are "appropriate" for specific people and practices and not others. Where people go, where they feel comfortable or out of place, and how they behave in certain environments all reflect the context of sociocultural and economic attitudes that have been sedimented in the landscape through time. These historical material landscapes and how people perform within them influence individuals in ways that are deep and unconscious—in effect forming or constituting them, their very identities and sense of self.

The insight that subjectivities are formed spatially is taken one step further by feminist theorists through an emphasis on interactivity and reflexivity. While it is evident that places greatly influence how people behave or perform within them, it is also clear that these places are similarly constituted and transformed through these practices. Thus we can see the mutual constitution of space and subjectivity—that while space "informs, limits and produces subjectivity," subjectivity at the same time "rearticulates certain historical definitions of space."[4]

Much of the work in geography focuses on constructions of gender and sexuality—how specific spaces are gendered and sexed, and how particular spaces (from a bar to a kitchen to a bathroom to a work space) produce ideologies of masculinity and femininity that force all of us to confront our gendered and sexed identifications and identities, but in unequal ways. Ideology and hegemony matter in these constructions. Those who feel comfortable and dominant in the space are able to "take" the space and further naturalize assumptions about who belongs and who does not, and how people ought to look and behave in it. They assert hegemonic ideals and narratives of masculinity and femininity that press upon and reach into bodies, recruiting and disciplining subjects at the same time.

Similar studies have been conducted on race and ethnicity, showing how space is raced as well as gendered and sexed. Mary Thomas's work on the spatiality of racial segregation in schools, for example, shows how the everyday spatial practices of teenagers reinscribe racial difference. Through their actions and narratives, the girls in her study shape and police racial boundaries. Even through banal spatial practices such as where they sit in the lunchroom, they perform hegemonic constructions of racial meaning. Through these repeated performances over time they are constituted as certain kinds of subject. Moreover, their practices help to (re)create the spatial conditions in which others act. In other words, they are part of the broader construction of a highly racialized socio-spatial field of action.[5]

It may seem like a closed loop, in which people's practices reflect their material and spatial conditions, and those conditions affect their practices and identities. Yet feminist theorists have argued for the importance of critical reflexivity as a way to escape—or at least become aware of—this cycle.[6] This type of reflexive awareness is only possible because of the multiple subject positions that constitute individuals (woman, lesbian, black, and so on) and the ways that everyday interaction, or life itself, always throws up contradictions and complications that can interrupt the hegemonic and iterative cycle. Although one can never completely step outside discourse, it is possible to see, learn, and become aware of the workings of ideology and hegemony—to some extent and in some domains—because of these uncomfortable disruptions to the smooth workings of "common sense" and "business as usual." These fracturing lines occur frequently throughout life, but at certain moments and times they can promote greater critical awareness and galvanize further political action.

Thus theories indicating the mutual constitution of ideology and subjectivity in real times and places, alongside the importance of critical reflection, are important in considering how people become political beings. Häkli and Kallio argue that political being and becoming, and corresponding acts of citizenship, occur as a result of both spatial attachments and personal connections rooted in specific places.[7] For them, citizenship acts should be contextualized both in terms of social relationships (topologies) and spatial relationships (topographies).

Political subjectivity and visibility and voice come through claiming space and through the construction of space in moments of crisis. Spatial crisis creates political actors. At the same time, acts of resistance create political spaces. What are some of the ways that this is manifested in the current era of neoliberal capitalism and education reform?

The Journey for Justice

Spatial crisis and political formation can be seen in contemporary struggles over schools and cities. Geographical awareness, knowledge, connection, and communication play a critical role in how parents and other social groups understand changes to their schools and neighborhoods, navigate local roadblocks and scale up their activism.

Instances of these forms of spatial and political activism in education are not difficult to find. In Seattle alone it is possible to point to several challenges to the reform coalition and its agenda. In response to the reforms pushed by the Broad Foundation-trained superintendent Goodloe-Johnson discussed in Chapter 6, for example, students, parents and teachers formed multiple alliances and successfully resisted many of the changes she instituted or attempted that were considered damaging to the community.

Integral to the alliances of resistance were two parents who formed a blog called Seattle Education 2010. The blog has received 1.2 million visitors since its establishment, and is now one of the foremost sources of information about the education reform agenda in the Pacific Northwest.[8] One of the parents, Sue Peters, subsequently ran successfully for a position as a school board director with Seattle Public Schools (SPS) from 2014 to 2018. The other, Dora Taylor, has written two books on education and joined the League of Women Voters King County Education Committee.

In addition to writing, campaigning, and organizing locally, the two scaled up their activism with the formation of the group Parents Across America, which now has chapters and affiliates in 26 states. Unlike the corporate "grassroots" campaigns such as Parent Trigger (widely derided as "Astroturf" movements), Parents Across America is "run by parents for parents" that seek to "share ideas and work together to strengthen and support our nation's public schools."[9] The agenda of the group is distinctly anti-reformist, with reflective, analytical positions countering high-stakes testing, school closures, school choice, and the privatization of public education.

The move from private citizens to public activists and from local concerns to national organizing occurred as a result of aggregate events coming together in space that helped to politicize the two women on this issue. Their journey to critical awareness about school closures and the choice movement in education accelerated as they made the spatial link between local and national scales. This is captured well in their "about us" introduction to the Seattle Education 2010 blog:

> When we began our blog, we were collecting information from many sources and trying to piece together the reasons for what was happening in our school system in Seattle in 2008 and 2009. We discovered that what was happening in Seattle was reflective of what was an attempt on a national level to transform public education. Only then did the actions of our superintendent in terms of school closures and program changes begin to make sense. We began to make the connections between Dr. Goodloe-Johnson, the Broad Foundation and charter schools and how that involved the Gates Foundation and ultimately the Race to the Top reform movement led by Education Secretary Arne Duncan. Our focus will still be to collect information regarding education and our goal will be to have an informed public on issues that affect us in Seattle in terms of education but it will now more consciously include looking at what is happening nationally and how that is affecting our public school system in Seattle.[10]

These kinds of scalar jumps are also evident in local Seattle movements to boycott unnecessary standardized tests, which became models for boycott movements nationally. Teachers at Garfield High School held a press conference in 2013 to announce the fact that they had voted unanimously to boycott the Measures of Academic Progress (MAP) test. Their decision not to administer the test was quickly backed by parents and students and joined by many other high schools in the city. By the end of the year, the SPS administration relented and the test no longer had to be administered to high-school students in the whole of Seattle.

The successful boycott made national news, with major news organizations such as NBC, NPR, and PBS all carrying the story. It then sparked resistance to high-stakes testing across the country.[11] In later press coverage about the growing movement, one of the founders, Jesse Hagopian, said in an interview, "I think that we have to see this movement against high-stakes standardized testing as a civil rights movement."[12]

Another national campaign that was sparked by local events and is emerging as a new civil rights struggle is Journey for Justice Alliance. Now with chapters in 24 cities across the United States, the grassroots alliance has been growing daily, carried forward initially by the rage and resistance at school closures in Chicago, and now an active, highly networked national movement. Journey for Justice is framed as a community movement, one that is run by and for the people most affected by school closures and the school choice movement: people of color. The reflective awareness of and resistance to the techniques of neoliberal governmentality, wherein African-American and Hispanic parents and students have been deliberately targeted as (necessary) choice-makers, is evident in many of the organization's public statements. For example, it states clearly on their website:

> We are not fooled by the "illusion of school choice." The policies of the last twenty years, driven more by private interests than by concern for our children's education, are devastating our neighborhoods and our democratic rights. Only by organizing locally and coming together nationally will we build the power we need to change local, state, and federal policy and win back our public schools.[13]

As a group that is not "fooled" by corporate reform, the alliance provides a good example of the many ways that targeted programs of improvement and rationalities of governance fail to connect up with the intended recipients. History and geography—the memory of schools as community anchors and the personal relations between local teachers and parents as something worth fighting for—enables people to see, learn about, and resist the neoliberal rationalities of freedom and choice. History and geography also provide the firm ground on which community actors can take a strong political stand.

The alliance, which deliberately makes connections with low-income, working-class communities, seeks to build "a national movement grounded in racial justice, education equity and building world-class sustainable community schools across the United States."[14] It is a political movement sustained by a long history of fighting spatial and racial injustice in cities such as Chicago, New Orleans, Atlanta, Philadelphia, and Detroit. How can the memories, goals, actors, and struggles of these types of movements become meaningful and alive to the next generation of youth?

Teaching critical geography to young people can galvanize a broader understanding of how spatial production has always been a critical part of uneven development—from resource extraction and gentrification to the exploitation of labor and people's emotional connections to place. It can also provide knowledge about historical commitments to community-building and resistance through time. In the following section I examine some of these historical forms of social inequity in Seattle, and how learning about and mapping the construction of neighborhoods over time can provide the foundations for present and future forms of democratic engagement and resistance to spatial injustice.

Social Justice Mapping with Children

In this mapping project I draw on research with middle-school children (aged 13 to 14) conducted with my former colleague, Sarah Elwood, in an independent (that is, fee-paying) girls' school from 2010 to 2011.[15] The school is in a relatively poor but rapidly gentrifying area of south Seattle. Some 45 percent of the students who participated identified themselves as non-white. Of the entire school population, 30 percent of the students received varying degrees of financial aid in the form of reduced tuition costs. The underlining premise of our research was that young people's increased awareness and understanding of spatial production—including the ways that individuals and groups have been included or excluded from society and space historically—can bring the knowledge and the desire to challenge inequity and social injustice in the present.

Our two-week mapping project dovetailed with a larger five-week project on the cultural history of Seattle. We worked with a social studies teacher and 29 seventh grade girls over several weeks, exploring the cultural histories of women and different ethnic and racial groups in the city. The girls formed teams of four students and each team chose to research a different group. These groups were women, Filipinos, Chinese, Japanese, and African-Americans. In a few cases the students were interested to find out more about their own ethnic history and so chose a group on that basis, but this was not the norm. Each team conducted interviews with local figures that were familiar with the history of the city or had been active in community-building and resistance projects over the past half century. They also talked with teachers and with us and used online and library-based resources to augment their knowledge. The teams then produced oral history video documentaries and interactive multimedia maps of important sites and spatial processes affecting the group that they researched.

To aid them in creating the maps we developed a web platform from open-source mapping and content management tools. This interactive environment enabled students to map and discuss the information, processes, and events they were researching. Important features included the ability of the students to add points, lines, and areas to the map, and append text or digital images to map objects. The collaborative function of the platform was enabled through a running "comment stream," where students could pose questions, respond to others, and add new information. One of the key questions we wanted to explore was whether a collaborative, experiential learning process was an important factor in facilitating geographic comprehension and encouraging democratic practices.[16]

In the project we asked in what ways a greater understanding of spatial production and management—such as through processes of mapping and counter-mapping—might provide the knowledge and skills to challenge inequitable resource allocation, segregation, gentrification, and other forms of spatial injustice. Three decades ago the famous cartographer and map historian Brian Harley noted that maps and mapmaking should always be viewed critically as tools that are generally at the disposal of dominant groups in society, and whose fundamental purpose is to "codify, to legitimate, and to promote the world views which are prevalent in different periods and places."[17] But although maps frequently uphold and advance dominant spatial and social norms and interests, they can also be produced in alternative ways for counter-hegemonic purposes.

Much critical research, for example, has demonstrated the usefulness of geographic information systems (GIS) in mapping populations usually rendered invisible and unacknowledged, such as recent immigrants and the homeless.[18] GIS is a method of using computers to store, display, visualize, and analyze spatial data. When tools such as GIS are in the right hands, populations such as these can benefit from being seen and counted in assessments of vulnerability and/or the need for social services. These types of studies recognize the embeddedness of maps in histories and geographies of power. They critique the notion of objectivity and neutrality in any mapping project. By the same token, they take into account the political possibilities inherent in modern geospatial technologies, actively and reflectively employing these tools in applied realms to further a critical politics of mapping against the grain.

Tate and Hogrebe have argued further that the highly visual nature of documentation provided by maps is important for underprivileged communities and a factor in higher rates of democratic participation.[19] In their work they examined, in particular, the intersection of visual computation tools, growing political awareness, and increased civic engagement. They argued that the more that relevant actors can see and manipulate visual data—such as layered digital maps showing inequitable spatial patterns—the greater likelihood those same actors would be able and willing to participate in an active and informed civic dialogue agitating for greater spatial equity.

Additionally, a significant amount of contemporary research in critical cartography has focused on the possibilities of an increasing democratization of knowledge and decision-making through the use of what has become known as participatory GIS. This body of work seeks to put the community at the center of community-building through collaborative public participation and experiential computer-mapping and analysis. It emphasizes bringing in a community-based perspective, and facilitating access to publicly available information so that shared knowledge can enable people to participate freely and in their own interests.

If marginalized community groups can derive power and authority from participatory geo-visualization technologies, what are the possibilities for children and young people? Four decades ago, the primary research on children's spatial awareness focused on questions of whether children's mapping abilities are innate or learned, and at what age they are able to comprehend spatial relationships and manifest them through various types of graphic representations. The geographer Jim Blaut argued that mapping ability reflects an atavistic survival mechanism universal to all human beings, and that children have an innate ability to trace, navigate, and represent space from very young ages.[20]

Piaget's influential work contrasted with Blaut by foregrounding developmental stages in children's understandings of space and geometry.[21] Drawing on this body of work, other scholars in psychology and education emphasized a notion of learned, developmental levels of competence in mapping rather than basic innate knowledge. In contrast to earlier work in geography by Blaut and his followers, these scholars argued for the importance of individual differences, and concepts of graduated learning dependent on levels of cognitive development. Although drawing on different literatures and emphasizing quite opposing viewpoints of learning and development, however, the two approaches shared a reliance on the individual as the key locus of mapping knowledge and ability. In other words, in both the nativist and the Piagetian traditions, children's spatial cognition was researched and understood on the basis of profoundly individual rather than social processes.

A third strand of research on children's spatial cognition focused on map-learning and awareness as part of a broader contextual world of social relationships and cultural communication. This body of work drew on the legacy of Lev Vygotsky, who promoted a view of schooling that foregrounded the social construction of knowledge and emphasized the context in which learning occurs.[22] For followers of Vygotsky, the collaborative and communicative process of mapping was of critical importance to understanding, as it is through the sharing of knowledge between more and less skilled children (and adults) that spatial relationships and cartographic concepts are best disseminated.[23]

Mapping History, Mapping Justice

In our participatory research we pursued the idea of social-justice mapping by introducing the seventh grade girls to counter-hegemonic thinking involving maps and cultural history. Research sessions were initiated with a discussion of the political importance of space, including teaching about how much of politics is often quite literally played out through the "taking" of space. For example, women and those categorized in various racial or ethnic groups often furthered their own political agendas through practices such as taking to the streets to demand the right to vote, or taking seats in buses, classrooms, and at lunch counters demanding the right to be served.

In these types of events, the narrow framing of the liberal public sphere as necessarily divided between normatively perceived issues that are "appropriate" for public discourse (issues purportedly related to the common good) versus those seen as "inappropriate" (supposedly private, individual) concerns is contested in and through space. Over time, historical practices of hatred and exclusion that have been bracketed as individual or private have permitted a kind of silent violence to be perpetrated on many marginalized groups in society. In recent years, this type of violence has been successfully contested through bringing these issues quite literally out into public space and thereby forcing them to become publicly recognized and debated.

These moments of challenge in the United States have included bringing into public visibility issues such as domestic violence, homophobia, and racism (and their multiple material effects, such as disenfranchisement,

segregation, and discrimination). The vaunted neutrality and inclusiveness of liberalism is thus put to the test when groups and individuals
take public space to manifest the multiple and ongoing exclusions that
the strict separation between public and private realms often produces
and maintains.

Helping young people understand the power of space can be initiated
through discussions and practices related to how communities have
lost or won space through the course of political struggle. Additionally,
students can be made more aware of how often marginalized communities
have held space in a manner affirming group identity through time. This
kind of approach to geography education advances a social justice or
emancipatory agenda, but it does so through the relatively simple means
of calling attention to certain kinds of spatial patterns, processes, and
relationships through time.

Questions about broader processes and patterns of spatial production
and control, and why particular events happened at particular locations,
elicit larger conceptual frameworks involving rights of association,
property, *habeas corpus*, and other civic and legal rights integral to
citizenship in the United States. When mapped and discussed within a
historical framework, students are able to quite literally see the abrogation
of key aspects of citizenship, through, for example, the internment of
Japanese Americans during World War II, or spatial patterns of institutionalized racism such as the redlining of minority neighborhoods. At
the same time, they can better visualize how subjugated communities
might be enhanced or protected through spatial proximity or access to
critical resources. Through discussion and further research, they can
also become aware of changes through time: changes that were often the
result of the activism of key figures, groups, or institutions asserting their
rights to particular spaces and resources.

We were interested in whether learning about these historical
processes would seem more immediate and important to students if they
could visualize how and where these things occurred in the neighborhoods where they live. The students involved in the project were asked to
investigate institutions such as immigrant enclaves, benevolent societies,
student unions, women's centers, and community headquarters as spaces
of social, political, and economic safety for historically marginalized or
terrorized groups. They also found evidence of exclusion and discrimination against these groups in processes such as redlining, steering,
internment, quarantining, and incarceration.

The mapping project was rooted in the proposition that place – specifically a reflective and critical knowledge about the places that are experienced in everyday life – could be a central catalyst in the development of political subjectivity and a commitment to political engagement. The study thus explored the link between a critical awareness of shared concerns and the development of a collective social awareness that might enhance civic agency and commitment to social and political action.

In each digital map created by the different teams, the students placed pins on areas of historical significance to their group. One of the teams investigating the historical geography of African-Americans in Seattle, for example pinned the location of the second Black Panther headquarters on their map. When the mapping platform was active, a viewer could click on a pin or on an area, and a comment box would pop up to the right. Often the students would add some textual description of the place, a photograph, or another related site for the viewer to visit. The conversations the students held about these pinned sites and corresponding text and photographs were mostly oral, but the researchers encouraged them to write some of their ideas into the comment box as well.

One student responded to a verbal question as to why there was a "second" Black Panthers headquarters by noting, "I think that the BPP [Black Panther Party] got evicted from some of their buildings and that's why they have multiple headquarters." This spurred another "why" question, followed by a response from the teacher. In these types of exchanges, the written comments were used to stimulate more oral dialogue, but they also provided a record of ideas, exchanges, and teaching moments that other students could see and react to at a later time or from a different place.

In another example from the team studying the historical geography of the Japanese in Seattle, a student mapped the Seattle Courthouse and explained why it was important to a university student named Hirabayashi. She noted how Hirabayashi "refused the evacuation," and in his legal defense invoked the Fifth Amendment in court. Students offered supportive comments after viewing the post. They also added additional information to the post, including a related website of interest. Significantly, one of the more advanced students in the class answered a direct question posed by the teacher about the Fifth Amendment's relevance to the internment struggles of Japanese-Americans. She showed her own understanding of the concept of due process, and at the same time helped the other students make further connections between the historical event of the internment and the idea of due process as a right guaranteed by the American Constitution.

In a third example, a student located a general area of the map (the International District) by using the line tool. She uploaded a photo from a main street in that neighborhood as a vehicle for talking about the practice of redlining. In her text, she introduced redlining in a somewhat confusing way: "Many Filipino people lived in the International District because it was the only place that wasn't redlined. Redlining is when basically an invisible line is put dividing where Filipinos can buy land." This prompted an oral question from a student outside the team, who had heard about it in relation to her own group's spatial formation and identity.

The comments that appeared in the text box following this dialogue demonstrated the collaborative, spatially-oriented learning process that occurred in the classroom as a result of this exchange. One student indicated her initial confusion about redlining with the question, "How did redlining actually work if it was like an invisible?" This was answered by the teacher, who used the student's question as a way of introducing the concept of restrictive covenants. Another student then brought in her own understanding of the process, which she had learned from her research on the Chinese experience in Seattle. She noted authoritatively, "Filipinos were not the only people who got redlined."

Democratic Participation and Engagement

By the fourth mapping session, Sarah and I observed that the students were thinking more critically and in more detail about the historical sites and social processes associated with the groups they were studying than they had earlier. In the first two sessions, most of the initial map objects were pitched at the neighborhood scale, with the historical cultural significance of the group articulated in very broad terms, sometimes even as simple as, "this is where Filipinos are." By the fourth session, however, the map content was becoming more complex and detailed—with notations on things like the activism of individuals, forms of group resistance, spatial processes such as internment, socioeconomic trans-formations such as women's entry into the industrial work force during

World War II, and gender stereotypes that led to women being tracked into particular sectors of the labor market.

The maps also picked up on the role of civic institutions both as a loci for activism or resistance and as sites for reinforcing cultural practices and community ties. Most of the teams included a cultural or community center such as the Japanese American Citizens' League, the NAACP (National Association of Advancement for Colored People), the Filipino Community Center, or a woman's association in the greater metro area. Several members of the teams were also passionate about demonstrating their knowledge of public space and public events as critical sites of protest.

In the fifth session, a student volunteer chose a point from another group's map, which was then projected onto a screen so that the entire class could see it. She read the text associated with that point, and one of the researchers facilitated a discussion to draw out historical and geographical connections or to introduce critical concepts. In this session, both the spatial thinking and the collaborative element of the sessions were clearly having an impact on the students. This was evident when many students began to make connections between the various forms of segregation experienced by the different groups.

We began by reviewing and commenting on a point on the team's map of the Filipino experience at Port Townsend, indicating where 339 Filipinos were quarantined in the late 1920s because of the "threat" of spinal meningitis. When the research team asked whether other minority or immigrant groups were also separated physically from the dominant society at some point in time, several hands went up, and many students talked about the experiences of the groups they had researched. For example, the team working on the Chinese experience talked about the Chinese Exclusion Act, telling us quite a bit about the social implications of these types of exclusions. Those researching the experiences of African-Americans spoke passionately about the redlining of their neighborhoods.

The main geographical connection that was made in the sixth session was the relationship between social relations of power and the formation of ethnic enclaves—particularly how groups might end up in a spatial cluster for various reasons, both positive and negative. In addition to the negative, external forces leading to enclaves such as restrictive covenants, some girls noted the importance of social groups advocating positively for their political rights as part of spatially concentrated organizations. Others, such as the team studying Filipinos, spoke about the importance of sociocultural feelings of membership, which might be achieved through ethnic clustering. We also questioned them about the potential economic advantages of being in an ethnic enclave, and many girls responded with ideas about spatial networks, retailing, and the importance of business nodes and links.

As is evident from these responses, many of the students used the mapping exercises as a way to inform themselves about both the geography and history of their own city and neighborhoods. Marking areas and sites of importance on their maps brought the cultural history of Seattle home to them, and helped them to add to their existing knowledge of the city. They began to see relationships between places, including where people live and where they work. On a broader regional scale, they began to see what it must have been like to have been quarantined or interned so far away from family and friends. This form of learning renders space and place socially contextualized in ways that bring geography to life, and makes it complementary to a broader democratic project of political activism and citizenship formation.

The students' growing interest in their own neighborhoods was manifested in some of the civic engagement worksheets that we had them fill in during the fifth session. Here the research team posed a number of questions related to social and spatial problems that each group had faced in Seattle. Three members of the team researching African-Americans responded to these questions by noting "redlining" and "discrimination," as well as the fact that "people couldn't get jobs because they were black."

To the question of what members of the community did to solve these problems, the students responded by giving specific examples of individual and community action, and also noted that all of these actions or processes had been represented on their map. In response to a final question about how their class or they personally might get involved in solving any remaining problems their group encountered, many students wrote specific things that they felt they could accomplish. Three girls wrote, for example, "Stalk the police and keep a tally of what races are pulled over and for what; Join the non-profit organizations."

Another group, which looked at the experience of Chinese Americans in Seattle, also described problems such as "laws that kept them from buying land (Alien Land Law), Exclusion Act, not allowed to be citizens until WWII." This group also named a specific person (Wing Luke) and organizations (the LELO, or Labor and Employment Law Office, the Chong Wa Benevolent Society, and the Chinese Information and Service Center) as people or institutions that had taken action to confront some of these problems. The two student members of the team also noted their own possible role in responding to ongoing problems for the community by indicating what they felt capable of: "Alerting people of these problems; Educating people; Video Documentary."

Making People's Geographers

In the collaborative mapping with middle-school students we found that a powerful alternative pedagogy was unleashed through spatial visualization. This geo-visualization included seeing the multiple ways that cultural history becomes layered and sedimented in the urban landscape. Importantly, these visible patterns were not perceived as something fixed and unchanging but rather as features of a process in constant motion and contestation.

Among the insights that the students derived, a key one was the understanding that both discriminatory actions such as redlining and the creation of affirmative locales such as the black student union are profoundly spatial processes critical in both scope and impact for historically subordinated groups. Literally placing people, institutions, and events in the students' own neighborhoods through locating them on a map of the city and attaching historical and contemporary documents to each mapped space helped them to graphically and visually connect both geography and history to the present time and place, and make it relevant to their own lives.

We employed the students' neighborhood awareness and urban geographies to draw out their own sense of place. The examples from participant observation, the students' maps, and the written and oral work presented here were selected to represent some of the spatial cognition and shared concerns that developed over the course of the two weeks. On the whole, we observed a growth in spatial awareness among the students as well as a strong concern about "spatial politics" related to the positive and negative geographical processes affecting group identity. Bringing together history, geography, and emancipatory politics through a collaborative mapping project helped the students to understand how minority communities are formed in and through space, and how important space is for maintaining solidarity and resisting oppression by dominant groups.

Further, through the process of researching, mapping, and talking with each other about their own city and neighborhoods, the students achieved a greater awareness that history is not necessarily a set of seemingly abstract events but rather is something that happened here, to us, in "our" space. Mapping "our" culture and "our" history can render events and processes more immediate, visceral, personal, and potentially alterable in terms of their seeming trajectory. Collectively visualizing and discussing historical acts such as the quarantining of Filipinos (there were two girls of Filipino descent in the class), or redlining in the African-American neighborhood where several of the girls lived, for example, seemed to galvanize a sense of collective responsibility for these spaces and the people who inhabit them.

In her work on New Orleans, Kristen Buras has written about the power of young people's counter-stories in challenging normative ideas about neoliberal market reform in the city.[24] Students opposed dominant white narratives by narrating the struggles and exposing the silences in the urban history of African-Americans and other minority communities. In a similar way, the middle-school students in this study used strategies of counter-mapping to resist hegemonic ways of representing space. They uncovered absences in the historical record and celebrated the multiple ways that women and minority groups had demanded and taken space in times past. Through this process, the students learned about and represented new spatial narratives of the city and, as young "people's geographers," they became political actors in their own right.

9

Conclusion: Paying Deep Attention

In this concluding chapter I think about education in a more holistic manner, reflecting on some of the ways that education also occurs outside of school. These forms of education include the learning that happens in sites and relationships beyond the classroom and also intergenerationally. In the previous chapter I highlighted the importance of spatial memory—how knowledge of community resistance and activism in times past can help young people become engaged citizens or "people's geographers" in the present. Here I want to extend this concept to thinking about spatial futures as well. How can children imagine future places, as well as the communities and geographies of the past, and how do the relationships between generations facilitate this? Further, how do these forms of spatial and temporal learning affect young people's growth, political development, and sense of self?

Thinking about temporal dimensions, as well as spatial ones, is useful as it can shed light on the ways that forms of collective memory—such as that about places or myths or historical events—are transmitted between generations. It is important to consider the transmission of collective memory from one generation to another as many believe it to be integral to a child's development of a strong sense of self. In his philosophical opus on time and technology, for example, the philosopher Bernard Stiegler contended that this process was vital for healthy subjectivity formation and for the development of responsible and mature adults.[1] He noted further that the transmission of collective memory between generations is currently under threat because of new "hyper" technologies. These are the types of technologies (such as social media) that constantly distract individuals and make it difficult, if not impossible, to pay deep and sustained attention to others.

Given the importance of intergenerational forms of education, what are some of the ways that radical geographies can help children to resist the allure of new technologies and pay deep attention? Our focus in the research project discussed below centered on the importance of historical memories of place and how they are captured and transmitted through maps, photos, poetry, and other types of cultural media. We were interested in how this archive of collective memory, transmitted inter-generationally both inside and outside the classroom, could galvanize new ways of paying attention and imagining possible places of the future. In order to locate some of these ideas in real times and places, we worked with young people to research, map, and write about the environmental and cultural histories, present conditions, and possible futures of two rivers in western Washington state.

Environmental Futures

The research project involved 13 fifth grade girls (ages 10 and 11) in an environmental science class. We worked with them and their teacher for several weeks over the course of the semester as they studied the Duwamish and Cedar rivers.[2] Both of these rivers drain into Puget Sound in Washington state.

The Duwamish has a history of heavy industrial use prior to environmental regulation, and in 2001 a five-mile stretch was put on the US Environmental Protection Agency's superfund list (an abatement program for severely polluted sites). As part of their environmental science and stewardship class, the students conducted conventional field science activities (water quality tests, species diversity studies, habitat observation) and interviewed a variety of contemporary stakeholders, including local government officials, volunteers and staff of local environmental NGOs, and members of the Native American Duwamish tribe. In parallel, we led a series of research, mapping, and writing activities in which the children examined the historical, environmental, and cultural processes behind these present-day conditions and activities, as well as writing about possible futures for the river.

The students' research, mapping, and writing generated a strong focus on the high levels of pollution and the frequently negative human interventions along the river during periods of intense and largely unregulated industrial use, from the late 1800s through the late 1900s. Relatedly, the students also researched and wrote about the preindustrial period, emphasizing the population of indigenous, native groups living there, and their everyday practices involving the river. Their explorations of the life of the river, including people who lived there from past to present, gave the young people a distinct sense of the passage of time. This was accompanied by a growing awareness of the many transformations to the landscape, as well as the negative impact on the Duwamish tribe that occurred as a result of interventions made by white settlers and engineers in the name of progress.

These understandings were made even more vivid as students began to map and discuss their research findings. On one map, for example, a student identified and marked a portion of the Duwamish that was dredged to allow for the passage of large ships. She annotated this marked area of the river with an old photograph showing heavy dredging machinery. Near this location on the river, another student placed a map pin and uploaded an old, historic map showing the meandering river course prior to nineteenth- and twentieth-century interventions. The dredging and other engineering projects were conducted to straighten the river for easier navigation, but they had a number of negative environmental ramifications vis-à-vis erosion and loss of habitat for wildlife. This was also a period of intense dispossession and dislocation for the Duwamish people.

Through these and other student contributions, the mapping afforded a space for critical learning and rethinking of normative historical narratives of industrial and technological "progress." When observed only in the present, the river simply "is," as if it has always been so, obscuring the processes through which this condition emerged. This collective effort to investigate and visualize the river's past alongside its present configuration and conditions, as in the juxtaposition of a map of the present-day river and the old map showing its twisting course a century ago, revealed the reality of intensive human intervention in the landscape. It challenges normative understandings of industry and technology as always progressive and positive, and foregrounds human–technological connections as often contradictory and sometimes having negative effects.

At one point in our work with them we read the students a poem by Richard Hugo about the Duwamish. Hugo grew up in White Center, a neighborhood of Seattle close to the river, and had seen and experienced many of its changes over time. In one stanza of the poem he depicted the dredging process, one that had also caught the students' attention in their own research and mapping.

> With salmon gone and industry moved in
> birds don't bite the water. Once this river
> brought a cascade color to the sea.
> Now the clouds are cod, crossing on the prowl
> beneath the dredge that heaps a hundred tons
> of crud on barges for the dumping ground.[3]

Toward the end of their project, we asked the students to write their own poem about the Duwamish. Many of the themes and images that Hugo had brought forth in his poem reverberated in interesting ways in their work, as did the stories, photos, figures, and maps that they had accessed throughout the semester. They wrote their poem collectively, with each student writing a line about the river's past, present, or future. One student's line in the poem, "I used to turn and twist, now I'm straight for freighter ships," indicated her own experience and imagination, but it was an image that was made possible via the collective historical memories that she and her classmates had accessed. This reflexive engagement of past and present through mapping, with an emphasis on the processes of change, also allowed an emergence of alternative futures. The students' poem continued by articulating long-term desires: "I hope to be a playground again," and sentiments towards future action: "We can do better."

These future imaginings spoke to the students' awareness of the connection of past to present and future, as well as humans' deep implication in processes of environmental change through time. Imagining an alternative future was made possible through access to an alternative past in the cultural archive of memory. This process was encouraged and mediated by educational relationships and through practices of mapping and writing.

In the examples from the fifth graders' river-mapping project, we can see that their engagement with past processes of human change transmits the notion of a future that might also become, emerge, and be actively remade through processes in which young people themselves might engage.[4] On several levels the poem manifested the students' incipient political formation through this process of connecting past, present, and future via mapping and writing. Many of the lines they contributed evoked a sense of loss, sadness, or regret about the river's degradation, together with a clear hope for a different future. These situated, emotional responses are central dimensions of spatial, political formation, potentially mobilizing the girls for future forms of democratic participation.

Other key elements of political formation were evident in the line "we can do better." This shows both a recognized agency in the world and a sense of membership in a collective "we" that indicates a willingness to intervene in environmental change in alternative ways. Awareness of broader power relations is critical, but so too is the belief that individuals can and indeed have made a difference in the past—and so might be able to do so in the future. While much work on children's political engagement has emphasized political acts, the formation of political subjects through spatial awareness, a sense of collective agency, and the experience of paying deep attention is a critically important part of this process.

The Spatial Politics of Erasure

The second example illustrates how mapping and writing can recover collective memory that has been lost or is excluded from normative historical accounts. At the same time, it can engender insight into the structural inequalities that underlie exclusion from the historical record. From their community interviews, the students knew that Native American groups have long been present in the area of the Duwamish and Cedar rivers. Yet in the course of their research they found little information about specific sites of historical importance along the river, and very limited visual and textual evidence of indigenous activities or uses of the river. Notably, nearly all their map objects related to Native American histories of the rivers emerged from their oral history interviews.

At first, the students charged with identifying and mapping indigenous histories of the Cedar and Duwamish rivers were deeply frustrated by the difficulty they experienced, several commenting "it's not fair" that their classmates responsible for mapping the industrial (almost exclusively white) histories of the rivers seemed to be finding evidence quite easily. Yet as the two groups worked to produce their collaborative map, they began to ask why these disparities existed, and to make connections between the uneven power relations that enabled white settlers to displace Native American residents, and at the same time to give them the literal power to write history. Very quickly, their narrative of unfairness shifted from their own research difficulties to the broader forms of persistent exclusion laid plain before them in the processes of mapping indigenous versus industrial histories.

In this research and mapping process, the students came to realize that the oral traditions that these indigenous communities used to pass on their own collective memories to the future had been disrupted. They came to recognize that the historical record is always partial and often inequitable. The ability to recognize such group-based inequalities, articulated through the children's own language as "not fair," constituted important beginnings of their political formation.

The critical insights into collective memory fostered through the students' reflexive engagement of writing and mapping also prompted them to re-examine connections between past and present, carried forward through the enduring legacies of spatial exclusion. For instance, in one annotation, a student narrated the recent struggles of the Duwamish tribe to gain federal recognition. With further research she and several classmates discovered that part of the rationale used by the government to deny the Duwamish claim of tribal status and territorial rights involved arguments that the group did not have a sustained presence in an identifiable and contiguous area. The girls immediately criticized this reasoning as unjust in light of the histories of forced displacement and dispossession experienced by the Duwamish throughout the nineteenth and into the twentieth century. How unfair, they retorted, to deny this claim on the basis of present-day "lack of cohesion" in the face of historical processes of exclusion and displacement. In this connection of past to present and present to past the students came to understand how processes of spatial exclusion created legacies of inequality that endure and have ongoing material repercussions through time.

The process of mapping provided these students with a space for critical reflection on the past, and a manner of connecting past and present in ways that manifested their contradictions and inequities. For these children, the seeds of political formation were sown in their emergent abilities to pay attention and to recognize collectively experienced inequalities and forces that inhibit coalition among marginalized groups.

Remaking Citizens

The philosophical framing and research illustrations of this chapter engaged questions of children's political formation through knowledge of time as well as space, and in the context of rapid technological changes alongside the transformations wrought by market-led globalization. In this era all subjects, including children, are faced with critical challenges related to the recent development of new hyper technologies. These technologies make paying deep attention increasingly difficult.

This is not an accident of history. Rather, it has to do with the *longue durée* of capitalist development, from the industrial period forward to our current era of short-term, consumer-oriented capitalism. In the face of this historical moment, the battle for young people's attention is at the same time a much broader struggle for the future of society.

In earlier parts of the book I looked at uneven development, divisions of labor, and new orientations to value and work under neoliberal forms of globalization. Global economic restructuring has led to contestations over nation, community, and work, the formation and reformation of citizenship, the closure and privatization of schools, and the understanding of what education should do and encompass. In this context, the epic struggles over education concern the vast amounts of capital accumulation made possible by privatization and dispossession. But they are also about the constitution of subjects as entrepreneurial, competitive, choice-making, economic beings. Indeed, some contemporary philosophers see the production of subjectivity as the most important enabler of *laissez-faire* capitalism.[5]

It is not surprising then, that education has become one of the most critical battlegrounds of the new millennium, with stakes that could not get much higher. Education reform has attracted multiple new actors including, most prominently, philanthropic foundations. These "stakeholders" have formed alliances with government and private-sector institutions in powerful new public–private partnerships bent on altering the terrain of public schooling worldwide. Their money and values are transforming the relationships and spaces of learning in myriad ways.

It is in this context of rapid and profound change that we must think about geographies of resistance. Many of the chapters in this book have pointed to the centrality of space in the processes of learning and work outlined here. And just as educational restructuring is located in spaces of uneven development, and the world of work is imbricated in new spatial divisions of labor, so too is resistance positioned in this wider geographical frame.

Remaking citizens is thus a geographical task. It is one that involves attention to the spaces of the past, and the ways that community members, academics, teachers, students, and activists have themselves formed alliances to take, protect, and cherish the places that are meaningful to them. It also involves dreams of the future, a geographical imagination that can counter neoliberal fantasies of planetary control, substituting these with visions of social and collaborative relationships. Radical geographies are collective hopes and concrete actions. They are people and places, connected by memory and imagination. Radical geographies are a manifesto for change.

Notes

Chapter 1

1. Paul Willis, *Learning to Labor: How Working Class Kids Get Working Class Jobs*, New York: Columbia University Press, 1977.
2. David Harvey, *The Limits to Capital*, Oxford: Blackwell, 1982.
3. Neil Smith, *Uneven Development: Nature, Capital, and the Production of Space*, Athens: University of Georgia Press, 1984.
4. Adam Smith, *The Wealth of Nations*, New York: Bantam Classics, 2003 [1776].
5. Doreen Massey, *Spatial Divisions of Labor: Social Structures and the Geography of Production*, London: Routledge, 1984.
6. Barry Bluestone and Bennett Harrison, *The Deindustrialization of America*, New York: Basic Books, 1984.
7. Matthew Sparke, *Introducing Globalization: Ties, Tensions, and Uneven Integration*, Oxford: Wiley-Blackwell, 2013, pp. 454–455.
8. Jamie Peck and Adam Tickell, "Neoliberalizing space," *Antipode* 34/3 (2002), pp. 380–404.
9. John Locke, *Two Treatises of Government*, London: Everyman, 1993 [1689].
10. Jeff Faux, "NAFTA's impact on US workers," Economic Policy Institute, December 9, 2013 (available at: http://www.epi.org/blog/naftas-impact-workers/, accessed May 3, 2017).
11. Laura Carlsen, "Under NAFTA, Mexico suffered and the United States felt its pain," *New York Times*, November 24, 2013 (available at: https://www.nytimes.com/roomfordebate/2013/11/24/what-weve-learned-from-nafta/under-nafta-mexico-suffered-and-the-united-states-felt-its-pain?mcubz=0/, accessed August 23, 2017).
12. David Bacon, "How US policies fueled Mexico's great migration," *The Nation*, January 4, 2012 (available at: https://www.thenation.com/article/how-us-policies-fueled-mexicos-great-migration/, accessed August 23, 2017).
13. Thomas Friedman, *The World Is Flat: A Brief History of the Twenty-First Century*, New York: Farrar, Straus, and Giroux, 2005.
14. David Harvey, "From managerialism to entrepreneurialism: The transformation in urban governance in late capitalism," *Geografiska Annaler Series B* 71/1 (1989), pp. 3–17.
15. Gordon MacLeod, "From urban entrepreneurialism to a 'revanchist city'? On the spatial injustices of Glasgow's renaissance," *Antipode* 34/3 (2002), pp. 602–624.

16. See, for example, William Tabb, *The Long Default: New York City and the Urban Fiscal Crises*, New York: Monthly Review Press, 1982.

17. Ronald McGuire, "The struggle at CUNY: Open admissions and civil rights," *SLAM! Herstory Project*, 1992 (available at: https://slamherstory.wordpress.com/2009/09/28/the-struggle-at-cuny-by-ron-mcguire/, accessed June 30, 2017). See also "1970–1977 open admissions—fiscal crisis—state takeover" (available at: http://cdha.cuny.edu/coverage/coverage/show/id/33, accessed June 30, 2017); and Michael Fabricant and Stephen Brier, *Austerity Blues: Fighting for the Soul of Public Higher Education*, Baltimore: Johns Hopkins University Press, 2016.

18. Thomas Mortenson, "State funding: A race to the bottom," *American Council on Education*, 2012 (available at: http://www.acenet.edu/the-presidency/columns-and-features/Pages/state-funding-a-race-to-the-bottom.aspx/, accessed May 3, 2017).

19. Ibid.

20. Patrick Cain, "University tuition fees in Canada rise 40 percent in a decade," *Global News*, September 7, 2016 (available at: http://globalnews.ca/news/2924898/university-tuition-fees-rise-40-per-cent-in-a-decade/, accessed June 27, 2017).

21. Richard Florida, *The Rise of the Creative Class: And How It's Transforming Work, Leisure, Community, and Everyday Life*, New York: Basic Books, 2003.

22. Jason Hackworth, *The Neoliberal City: Governance, Ideology, and Development in American Urbanism*, Ithaca, NY: Cornell University Press, 2006.

23. Adrian Smith, "Gentrification and the spatial constitution of the state: The restructuring of London's Docklands," *Antipode* 21/3 (1989), pp. 232–260.

24. Preliminary statistics show a drop in the numbers of EU nationals working in the UK since the Brexit vote. See Gemma Tetlow, "Number of EU nationals working in the UK starts to fall," *Financial Times*, February 15, 2017 (available at: https://www.ft.com/content/1e5d5330-f37f-11e6-8758-687615182166/, accessed August 23, 2017).

25. See Daniel Bessner and Matthew Sparke, "Don't let his trade policy fool you: Trump is a neoliberal," *Washington Post*, March 22, 2017 (available at: https://www.washingtonpost.com/posteverything/wp/2017/03/22/dont-let-his-trade-policy-fool-you-trump-is-a-neoliberal/?utm_term=.466a79c38c51/, accessed August 23, 2017).

26. These include opportunities such as the student exchange program Erasmus (European Region Action Scheme for the Mobility of University Students) and labor mobility programs such as EaSI (Employment and Social Innovation).

27. World Bank statistics indicate that officially recorded remittances to developing countries (which are far less than the actual amounts of money transfers) were $427 billion in 2014. The highest numbers of remittances went to China, the Philippines, and Mexico. See World Bank, "Migration overview" (available at: http://www.worldbank.org/en/topic/migration remittancesdiasporaissues/overview/, accessed May 3, 2017).

28. Katharyne Mitchell and Key MacFarlane, "Crime and the global city: Migration, borders and the pre-criminal," Oxford Handbooks Online, Oxford: Oxford University Press, 2016 (available at: http://www.oxfordhandbooks.com/view/10.1093/oxfordhb/9780199935383.001.0001/oxfordhb-9780199935383-e-45/, accessed August 23, 2017).

29. Rachel Silvey, "Geographies of gender and migration: Spatializing social difference," *International Migration Review* 40/1 (2006) pp. 64–81.

30. See, for example, Pia Orrenius and Madeline Zavodny, "Do immigrants work in riskier jobs?" *Demography* 46/3 (2009) pp. 535–551.

31. Phillip Brown, Hugh Lauder, and David Ashton, *The Global Auction: The Broken Promises of Education*, Oxford: Oxford University Press, 2011.

32. Ibid., pp. 148–149.

Chapter 2

1. See, for example, Michel Foucault, *The Birth of Biopolitics: Lectures at the Collège de France, 1978–1979*, London: Picador, 2010. Foucault did not use the term neoliberalism but he was one of the earliest scholars to identify many of its characteristics.

2. Foucault, *Biopolitics*.

3. Gary Becker, *The Economic Approach to Human Behavior*, Chicago: University of Chicago Press, 1976.

4. Nikolas Rose, *Powers of Freedom: Reframing Political Thought,* Cambridge: Cambridge University Press, 1999.

5. Ibid., p. 214.

6. Thomas Friedman, *The Lexus and the Olive Tree: Understanding Globalization*, New York: Farrar, Strauss, and Giroux, 1999.

7. Nikolas Rose and Carlos Novas, "Biological citizenship," in Aihwa Ong and Stephen Collier (eds), *Global Assemblages: Technology, Politics, and Ethics as Anthropological Problems*, Oxford: Wiley-Blackwell, 2004, pp. 439–463.

8. Matthew Sparke, "Austerity and the embodiment of neoliberalism as ill-health: Towards a theory of biological sub-citizenship," *Social Science and Medicine* 187 (2017), pp. 287–295.

9. Craig Jeffrey, Patricia Jeffery, and Roger Jeffery, *Degrees without Freedom? Education, Masculinities, and Unemployment in North India*, Stanford: Stanford University Press, 2007, p. 2.

10. Ann Anagnost, "The corporeal politics of quality (suzhi)," *Public Culture* 16/2 (2004), pp. 189–208.

11. Cindi Katz, *Growing up Global: Economic Restructuring and Children's Everyday Lives*, Minneapolis: University of Minnesota Press, 2005.

12. Aid to Families with Dependent Children and Head Start were among the many US programs affected by the rapid withdrawal of federal funding during this period. A lingering result of this revanchist attack on social provisioning is that one in five children in the United States now lives in poverty, an increase of 13 percent between 2000 and 2005 alone. In 2013, 2.5 million children and youth were homeless. See National Center for Children

in Poverty (available at: http://www.nccp.org/topics/childpoverty.html/, accessed May 15, 2017). See also Ellen Bassuk, Carmela DeCandia, Corey Beach, and Fred Berman, "America's Youngest Outcasts: A Report Card on Child Homelessness," American Institutes for Research, 2014 (available at: https://www.air.org/sites/default/files/downloads/report/Americas-Youngest-Outcasts-Child-Homelessness-Nov2014.pdf, accessed August 20, 2017).

13. Katz, *Growing up Global*, p. 163.

14. For the United States, see Kim Blakely, "Parents' conceptions of social danger to children in the urban environment," *Children's Environments* 11/1 (1994) pp. 16–25; for the United Kingdom, see Gill Valentine and John McKendrick, "Children's outdoor play: Exploring parental concerns about children's safety and the changing nature of childhood," *Geoforum* 28/2 (1997) pp. 219–235.

15. See, for example, the case of Alexander and Danielle Meitiv, whose children (ages ten and six) were twice picked up by the police and taken into the custody of the Child Protective Services after they walked home together from a park. The parents were charged with child neglect, but both cases were eventually dropped. See Donna St. George, "'Free range' parents cleared in second neglect case after kids walked alone," *Washington Post*, June 22, 2015 (available at: https://www.washingtonpost.com/local/education/free-range-parents-cleared-in-second-neglect-case-after-children-walked-alone/2015/06/22/82283c24-188c-11e5-bd7f-4611a60dd8e5_story.html?utm_term=.da5dc65654e5/, accessed August 24, 2017).

16. Rice was with his 14-year-old sister at the time. She was forced to the ground and handcuffed after she ran to her brother's aid.

17. Institute for Social Research, University of Michigan (available at: http://home.isr.umich.edu/, accessed May 2, 2017).

18. Richard Louv, *Last Child in the Woods: Saving Our Children from Nature-Deficit Disorder*, Chapel Hill, NC: Algonquin Books, 2005.

19. David Elkind, *The Power of Play: How Spontaneous Imaginative Activities Lead to Happier, Healthier Children*, Cambridge, MA: Da Capo Press, 2007.

20. See, for example, Frederick Zimmerman, Dimitri Christakis, and Andrew Meltzoff, "Associations between media viewing and language development in children under 2 years," *Journal of Pediatrics* 151/4 (2007) pp. 364–368.

21. Annette Lareau, *Unequal Childhoods: Class, Race, and Family Life*, Berkeley: University of California Press, 2003.

22. Rebecca Callahan and Patricia Gándara, *The Bilingual Advantage: Language, Literacy and the US Labor Market*, Bristol: Multilingual Matters, 2014, p. 10.

23. John Stanford Elementary School, "Our Vision" (available at: http://stanfordes.seattleschools.org/about, accessed May 2, 2017).

24. Walter Parker, "'International education' in US public schools," *Globalisation, Societies and Education* 9/3–4 (2011) pp. 487–501.

25. National Academy of Sciences, National Academy of Engineering, and Institute of Medicine, *Rising Above the Gathering Storm: Energizing and*

Employing America for a Brighter Economic Future, Washington: National Academies Press, 2007.

26. National Commission on Excellence in Education, "A Nation at Risk: The Imperative of Educational Reform," report to the Secretary of Education, United States Department of Education, April, 1983.

27. Anne Case and Angus Deaton, "Mortality and morbidity in the 21st century," Brookings Panel on Economic Activity, 2017 (available at: https://www.brookings.edu/wp-content/uploads/2017/03/casedeaton_sp17_finaldraft.pdf/, accessed 18 June, 2017).

28. Michelle Alexander, *The New Jim Crow: Mass Incarceration in the Age of Colorblindness,* New York: New Press, 2010.

29. Liu Wei Hua and Zhang Xin Wu, *Harvard Girl Liu Yiting: Documentary on Quality Training* (in Chinese), Beijing: Writers Publishing House, 2009.

30. See, for example, some of the materials on international student recruiting from Intead: International Education Advantage, LLC (available at http://intead.com/, accessed July 7, 2017).

Chapter 3

1. See, for example, Michael Sanderson, *Education, Economic Change and Society in England, 1780–1870,* London: Macmillan, 1983.

2. Samuel Bowles and Herbert Gintis, *Schooling in Capitalist America: Educational Reform and the Contradictions of Economic Life,* Chicago: Haymarket Books, 1976.

3. Paul Willis, *Learning to Labor: How Working Class Kids Get Working Class Jobs,* New York: Columbia University Press, 1981.

4. Andy Green, *Education and State Formation: The Rise of Educational Systems in England, France and the USA,* New York: St. Martin's Press, 1990.

5. There are numerous studies of the ways that narratives of multicultural tolerance have been used to elide or deny the ongoing practices of state-based racism in anglophone settler societies. For Canada, see, for example, Eva Mackey, *The House of Difference: Cultural Politics and National Identity in Canada,* Toronto: University of Toronto Press, 2002; and Richard Day, *Multiculturalism and the History of Canadian Diversity,* Toronto: University of Toronto Press, 2000.

6. Katharyne Mitchell, *Crossing the NeoLiberal Line: Pacific Rim Migration and the Metropolis,* Philadelphia: Temple University Press, 2004.

7. Neil McDonald, "Egerton Ryerson and the school as an agent of political socialization," in Neil McDonald and Alf Chaiton (eds), *Egerton Ryerson and His Times,* Toronto: Macmillan, 1978, pp. 81–106.

8. Quebec and Newfoundland were the two exceptions here, representing the most divergent positions from this otherwise fairly broad liberal hegemony.

9. The quote is from the nineteenth-century educational superintendent of Ontario, Egerton Ryerson, cited by Ronald Manzer, *Public Schools and Political Ideas: Canadian Educational Policy in Historical Perspective,* Toronto: University of Toronto Press, 1994, p. 76.

10. Egerton Ryerson, "Report on a system of public elementary instruction for Upper Canada," in John George Hodgins (ed.), *Documentary History of Education in Upper Canada, 1791–1876*, Toronto: King's Printer, 1901.

11. See Andrew Armitage, *Social Welfare in Canada Revisited: Facing Up to the Future*, Toronto: Oxford University Press, 1996; Mary Ruggie, *Realignments in the Welfare State: Health Policy in the United States, Britain, and Canada*, New York: Columbia University Press, 1996.

12. These reports were: George Radwanski, "Ontario Study of the Relevance of Education, and the Issue of Dropouts," Toronto: Ministry of Education, 1987; and Barry Sullivan, "A Legacy for Learners: The Report of the Royal Commission on Education 1988," Victoria: Queen's Printer for British Columbia, 1988.

13. Radwanski, "Ontario Study," p. 38. See also Jerry Paquette, "Equity in educational policy: A priority in transformation or in trouble?" in Stephen Ball, Ivor Goodson, and Meg Maguire (eds), *Education, Globalisation and New Times*, London: Routledge, 2007, pp. 335–360. Following the publication of these reports, a number of provinces began to follow suit with similar types of reports and campaigns. See, for example, the reports of the Ontario Premier Council, "Competing in the New Global Economy," 1988; and "People and Skills in the New Global Economy," 1990; and the report of the Economic Council of Canada, "A Lot to Learn: Education and Training in Canada", Ottawa: Minister of Supply and Services Canada, 1992. See also the New Brunswick, Commission on Excellence in Education, "Schools for a New Century," Fredericton: Commission on Excellence in Education, 1992. These reports and documents and the kind of policy shift they imply are insightfully analyzed by Manzer, *Public Schools and Political Ideas*, pp. 212–237.

14. See, for example, the consultative paper put together by various federal ministers, Canada, Prosperity Secretariat, "Living Well … Learning Well," Ottawa: Minister of Supply and Services Canada, 1991.

15. Christopher Lubienski and Ee-Seul Yoon, "Introduction to the special issue: Studying school choice in Canada," *Education Policy Analysis Archives* 25/37 (2017), p. 7. See all of the articles in this special issue for an informed look at the impact of neoliberal policy on the contemporary education system in Canada.

16. Green, *Education and State Formation*.

17. Richard Tawney, "Equality," reprinted in Harold Silver (ed.), *Equal Opportunity in Education: A Reader in Social Class and Educational Opportunity*, London: Methuen, 1973, pp. 29–63. For the postwar period, see Brian Jackson and Dennis Marsden, *Education and the Working Class*, London: Penguin, 1969.

18. Ken Jones, *Education in Britain: 1944 to the Present*, Cambridge: Polity Press, 2016.

19. Dawn Gill, Barbara Mayor, and Maud Blair, *Racism and Education: Structures and Strategies*, London: Sage, 1994.

20. Barry Troyna, *Racism and Education*, Buckingham: Open University Press, 1993.

21. Tariq Modood and Stephen May, "Multiculturalism and education in Britain: An internally contested debate," *International Journal of Educational Research* 31 (2001), pp. 305–317.

22. This was a speech decrying the negative impact of black immigration on the cultural values and traditions of Britain. See Enoch Powell, "Rivers of Blood," speech given at the Conservative Political Centre in Birmingham, England, April 20, 1968 (available at: https://www.youtube.com/watch?v= mw4vMZDItQo, accessed July 11, 2017).

23. Jones, *Education in Britain*, p. 108.

24. For a general analysis of the Thatcher government's attack on welfarism in England and the introduction and expansion of neoliberalism, see Stuart Hall, "The toad in the garden: Thatcherism among the theorists," in Cary Nelson and Lawrence Grossberg (eds), *Marxism and the Interpretation of Culture*, Chicago: University of Illinois Press, 1988, pp. 35–73.

25. Hall, "The toad in the garden"; Paul Gilroy, *There Ain't No Black in the Union Jack: The Cultural Politics of Race and Nation*, Chicago: University of Chicago Press, 1987.

26. Quoted in Jonathan Rutherford, "Uncreative friendship," *Times Higher Education*, April 27, 2001 (available at https://www.timeshighereducation. com/news/uncreative-friendship/159390.article/, accessed August 29, 2017).

27. Jones, *Education in Britain*, p. 172.

28. Green, *Education and State Formation*.

29. Joel Spring, *Deculturalization and the Struggle for Equality: A Brief History of the Education of Dominated Cultures in the United States*, New York: Routledge, 2016.

30. Carl Kaestle, *Pillars of the Republic: Common Schools and American Society 1780–1860*, New York: Hill and Wang, 1983; Bowles and Gintis, *Schooling in Capitalist America*.

31. This case challenged the 1896 Supreme Court case, *Plessy v. Ferguson*, which upheld the policy of "separate but equal" in all public establishments including schools.

32. James Banks and Cherry Banks (eds), *Handbook of Research on Multicultural Education*, New York: Macmillan, 1995.

33. John Dewey, *Democracy and Education: An Introduction to the Philosophy of Education*, New York: Macmillan, 1916, p. 99.

34. Theresa Perry and Jim Fraser, *Freedom's Plow: Teaching in the Multicultural Classroom*, New York: Routledge, 1993.

35. Nikhil Singh, *Black is a Country: Race and the Unfinished Struggle for Democracy*, Cambridge, MA: Harvard University Press, 2005.

36. James Banks and Cherry Banks (eds), *Multicultural Education: Issues and Perspectives*, Hoboken, NJ: John Wiley and Sons, 2013.

37. National Commission on Excellence in Education, "A Nation at Risk: The Imperative of Educational Reform," report to the Secretary of Education, United States Department of Education, April, 1983.

38. Task Force on Education for Economic Growth, "Action for Excellence: A Comprehensive Plan to Improve our Nation's Schools," Denver, CO: Denver Education Commission of the States, 1983, p. 23.

39. Chester Finn, "A call for quality education," *American Education*, January–February, 1982, p. 32.

40. Stanley Aronowitz and Henry Giroux, *Education Under Siege: The Conservative, Liberal and Radical Debate over Schooling*, Cambridge, MA: Bergin and Garvey, 1985.

41. George Bush, "Foreword," January, 2002 (available at: https://georgewbush-whitehouse.archives.gov/news/reports/text/no-child-left-behind.html/, accessed May 4, 2017).

Chapter 4

1. Marjan Šimenc and Zdenko Kodelja, "Lifelong Learning—From Freedom to Necessity," *Creative Education* 7 (2016), pp. 1714–1715.

2. UNESCO, "Final Report: Third International Conference on Adult Education, Tokyo, 25 July–7 August 1972" (available at: http://www.unesco.org/education/uie/confintea/tokyo_e.pdf/, accessed August 30, 2017).

3. See, for example, Šimenc and Kodelja, "Lifelong Learning."

4. See Paul Lengrand, *An Introduction to Lifelong Education*, Paris: UNESCO, 1975 [1970]; Dennis Kallen and Jarl Bengtsson, *Recurrent Education: A Strategy for Lifelong Learning*, Washington: OECD, 1973.

5. Kallen and Bengtsson, *Recurrent Education*, pp. 42–43.

6. This concept is generally associated with the political-economic works of Karl Marx, who theorized the existence of a reserve army of labor as a necessary condition for the successful organization of work in a capitalist system.

7. Katherine Nicoll and Henning Salling Olesen, "Editorial: What's new in a new competence regime?" *European Journal for Research on the Education and Learning of Adults* 4/2 (2013), p. 104.

8. UK Department for Education and Employment, "The Learning Age: A Renaissance for a New Britain," London: Stationery Office, 1998.

9. US Congress, Taxpayer Relief Act of 1997, sec. 201 (available at: https://www.gpo.gov/fdsys/pkg/PLAW-105publ34/html/PLAW-105publ34.htm/, accessed 20 May 2017); Department of Finance Canada, "The Budget Plan 1998," Ottawa: Her Majesty the Queen in Right of Canada, 1998.

10. UK Department for Education and Employment, "The Learning Age", sec. 1.16.

11. Jane Cruikshank, "Lifelong learning and the new economy: Rhetoric or reality?" *Education Canada* 47/2 (2007), pp. 32–36.

12. Tara Gibb and Judith Walker, "Educating for a high skills society? The landscape of federal employment, training and lifelong learning policy in Canada," *Journal of Education Policy* 26/3 (2011), p. 381.

13. Lisa Philipps, "Registered savings plans and the making of middle class Canada: Toward a performative theory of tax policy," *Fordham Law Review* 84/6 (2016), p. 2693.

14. Michael Mumper, "The future of college access: The declining role of public higher education in promoting equal opportunity," *Annals of the American Academy of Political and Social Science* 585 (2003), p. 108.

15. Philipps, "Registered savings plans," p. 2693.

16. See John T. Addison, "Labor policy in the EU: The new emphasis on education and training under the Treaty of Amsterdam," *Journal of Labor Research* 23/2 (2002), p. 308.

17. European Commission, "Towards a Europe of knowledge," communication from the Commission to the Council, the European Parliament, the Economic and Social Committee and the Committee of the Regions. COM (97) 563 final, November 12, 1997 (available at: http://aei.pitt.edu/5546/1/5546.pdf/, accessed May 25, 2017).

18. European Commission, "A European area of lifelong learning: empowering Europeans in the knowledge-based economy and society," European Commission Press Release Database, November 21, 2001 (available at: http://europa.eu/rapid/press-release_IP-01-1620_en.htm/, accessed May 18, 2017).

19. Lisbon European Council, "Presidency conclusions," March 23 and 24, 2000 (available at: http://www.europarl.europa.eu/summits/lis1_en.htm/, accessed May 12, 2017).

20. Ibid.

21. John Holford and Vida Mohorčič Špolar, "Neoliberal and inclusive themes in European lifelong learning policy," in Sheila Riddell, Jörg Markowitsch, and Elisabet Weedon (eds), *Lifelong Learning in Europe*, Bristol: Policy Press, 2012, pp. 39–61; see also Roger Dale and Susan Robertson, *Globalisation and Europeanisation in Education*, Providence, RI: Symposium Books, 2009.

22. Susan Robertson, "Europe, competitiveness and higher education: An evolving project," in Robert Dale and Susan Robertson (eds), *Globalisation and Europeanisation in Education*, Providence, RI: Symposium Books, 2009, pp. 65–83.

23. Peter Drucker, *The Changing World of the Executive*, London: Routledge, 2011 [1982], p. 112.

24. Richard Florida, *Cities and the Creative Class*, New York: Routledge, 2004.

25. Jamie Peck, "Struggling with the creative class," *International Journal of Urban and Regional Research* 29/4 (2005), pp. 740–770.

26. Kate Oakley and David O'Brien, "Learning to labour unequally: Understanding the relationship between cultural production, cultural consumption and inequality," *Social Identities: Journal for the Study of Race, Nation and Culture* 22/5 (2016), p. 474.

27. Wendy Brown, *Regulating Diversion: Tolerance in the Age of Identity and Empire*, Princeton: Princeton University Press, 2008.

28. Peter Drucker, *Managing for Results*, London: Routledge, 2011 [1964] p. 208.

29. Peter Drucker, "Worker and work in the metropolis," *Daedalus* 97/4 (1968), p. 1251.

30. Karl Marx, *Capital: A Critique of Political Economy*, Vol. 1, New York: Penguin, 1990, p. 449.
31. Ibid.
32. Nigel Thrift, *Knowing Capitalism*, London: Sage, 2005, p. 93.
33. Michael Burawoy, *Manufacturing Consent: Changes in the Labor Process under Monopoly Capitalism*, Chicago: University of Chicago Press, 1979, p. 120.
34. Antonio Gramsci, *Selections from the Prison Notebooks*, New York: International Publishers, 1971.

Chapter 5

1. John Dewey, *Democracy and Education*, New York: Macmillan, 1924.
2. T.H. Marshall, "Citizenship and Social Class" [1950], in T.H. Marshall and Tom Bottomore, *Citizenship and Social Class*, London: Pluto Press, 1992, part I.
3. Michael Mann, "Ruling class strategies and citizenship," *Sociology* 21/3 (1987), pp. 339–354.
4. Bryan Turner, "Outline of a theory of citizenship," *Sociology* 24/2 (1990), pp. 189–217.
5. Uday Singh Mehta, *Liberalism and Empire: A Study in Nineteenth-Century British Liberal Thought*, Chicago: University of Chicago Press, 1999.
6. Aihwa Ong, "Cultural citizenship as subject-making," *Current Anthropology* 37/5 (1996), pp. 737–762.
7. The concept of deterritorialization comes from Gilles Deleuze and Félix Guattari, *Anti-Oedipus: Capitalism and Schizophrenia*, trans. Robert Hurley, London: Continuum, 2004.
8. Walter Parker, "'International education' in US public schools," *Globalisation, Societies and Education* 9/3–4 (2011), pp. 487–501.
9. Aihwa Ong, *Flexible Citizenship: The Cultural Logic of Transnationality*, Durham, NC: Duke University Press, 1999, p. 4.
10. Cecilia Kalaw, Arlene McLaren, and Nadene Rehnby, "In the name of choice—A study of traditional schools in BC," *Canadian Centre for Policy Alternatives*, June 1998, p. 4.
11. May Leung, "Letter to the editor," *Richmond News*, May 13, 1998, p. 11.
12. S. O'Connell, "Letter to the editor," *Richmond News*, June 14, 1998, p. 11.
13. E. Parper, "Letter to the editor," *Richmond News*, May 10, 1998, p. 11.
14. Those selected were culled from 21 published letters to the editor on the issue that were sent to the *Richmond News* between March and July 1998. They are generally representative of the types of schisms that were aired in the community during this time, although numerous other issues pertaining to traditional schools were also raised.
15. This quote is from Reuban Chan, the committee chair at the meetings.
16. There were ten round tables at the meeting, with eight to ten people at each table, each representing different schools within the Richmond school district. Notably, none of the traditional-school proponents participated in

these public meetings. I was told by several people that the traditional-school advocates felt that their needs were not being addressed by the Foundations Program concept and thus they declined to attend.

17. The viewpoint expressed here was corroborated in a number of interviews with Chinese traditional-school proponents conducted in 1998.

18. Wendy Brown, *Regulating Aversion: Tolerance in the Age of Identity and Empire*, Princeton: Princeton University Press, 2006.

Chapter 6

1. Jamie Peck, *Constructions of Neoliberal Reason*, Oxford: Oxford University Press, 2010.

2. Katharyne Mitchell and Matthew Sparke, "The new Washington consensus: Millennial philanthropy and the making of global market subjects," *Antipode* 48/3 (2016), pp. 724–749.

3. See William Watkins, *The White Architects of Black Education: Ideology and Power in America, 1865–1877*, New York: Teacher's College Press, 2001.

4. First chairman of Rockefeller's General Education Board, quoted in Waldemar Nielsen, *The Big Foundations: A Twentieth Century Fund Study*, New York: Columbia University Press, 1972, p. 335.

5. The phrase "life themselves" is taken from the Gates Foundation website: "Guided by the belief that every life has equal value, the Bill & Melinda Gates Foundation works to help all people lead healthy, productive lives. In developing countries, it focuses on improving people's health and giving them the chance to lift themselves out of hunger and extreme poverty" (available at: https://www.gatesfoundation.org/Who-We-Are/General-Information/Foundation-Factsheet/, accessed August 30, 2017).

6. Katherine Rankin, "Governing development: Neoliberalism, microcredit, and rational economic woman," *Economy and Society* 30/1 (2001), pp. 18–37.

7. Jonathan Kozol, *Savage Inequalities: Children in America's Schools*, New York: Broadway Books, 1991; and *The Shame of the Nation: The Restoration of Apartheid Schooling in America*, New York: Broadway Books, 2005.

8. National Commission on Excellence in Education, "A Nation at Risk: The Imperative of Educational Reform," report to the Secretary of Education, United States Department of Education, April, 1983.

9. Diane Ravitch, *The Death and Life of the Great American School System*, New York: Basic Books, 2010.

10. Charter schools are publicly funded but privately run. They are often managed by for-profit charter management organizations (CMOs) and can negatively impact the regular public school system through loss of revenue. Each state has a different set of rules and regulations governing charter schools, with some states more interested in adopting and promoting them than others. Overall, the national trend is strongly pro-charter.

11. For one example, see Kate Menken, "Teaching to the test: How No Child Left Behind impacts language policy, curriculum, and instruction for

English language learners," *Bilingual Research Journal* 30/2 (2006), pp. 521–546.

12. Linda Darling-Hammond, "Race, inequality and educational accountability: The irony of 'No Child Left Behind," *Race, Ethnicity and Education* 10/3 (2007), pp. 245–260.

13. Theoni Soublis Smyth, "Who is No Child Left Behind leaving behind?" *Clearing House: A Journal of Educational Strategies, Issues and Ideas* 81/3 (2008), pp. 133–137.

14. Henry Giroux, *The Terror of Neoliberalism: Authoritarianism and the Eclipse of Democracy*, London: Paradigm, 2004, p. 37.

15. Joe Onosko, "'Race to the Top' leaves children and future citizens behind: The devastating effects of centralization, standardization, and high stakes accountability," *Democracy and Education* 19/2 (2011), pp. 1–11

16. Tina Trujillo and Kenneth Howe, "Weighing the effects of federal educational policy on democracy: Reframing the discourse on high-stakes accountability," *Teachers College Record* 117/6 (2015), pp. 1–6.

17. Gates Foundation, "The Bill and Melinda Gates Foundation commits $25.9 million to the Alliance for Education and Seattle Public Schools to help all children achieve in the classroom," press release, 1 March 2000.

18. See, for example, Linda McGoey's discussion of the disastrous outcome for Denver's Manual High School in *No Such Thing as a Free Gift: The Gates Foundation and the Price of Philanthropy*, New York: Verso, 2015.

19. Kenneth Saltman, *The Gift of Education: Public Education and Venture Philanthropy*, Basingstoke: Palgrave Macmillan, 2010, p. 80.

20. Ibid., p. 82.

21. Race-based or "forced" busing in the United States involved transporting students to non-local schools in an effort to desegregate neighborhood school systems, which were often highly segregated by race owing to the effects of residential segregation.

22. John Stanford, *Victory in Our Schools: We Can Give Our Children Excellent Public Education*, New York: Bantam, 1999.

Chapter 7

1. Milton Friedman, "Busting the school monopoly," *Newsweek*, December 5, 1983, p. 96.

2. *Won't Back Down*, Daniel Barnz (dir.), Twentieth-Century Fox, 2012, 121 mins.

3. *Waiting for "Superman"*, Davis Guggenheim (dir.), Paramount, 2010, 102 mins. Several other documentaries disparaging public education appeared around the same time. These included *The Lottery* (2010), which attacked public education and promoted charter schools; *Teached* (2011), by a former member of Teach for America; and *The Cartel* (2009).

4. Diane Ravitch, *Reign of Error: The Hoax of the Privatization Movement and the Danger to America's Public Schools*, New York: Alfred Knopf, 2013.

5. Joanne Barkan, "Hired guns on astroturf: How to buy and sell school reform," *Dissent*, spring 2012 (available at: https://www.dissentmagazine.org/article/hired-guns-on-astroturfhow-to-buy-and-sell-school-reform/, accessed September 1, 2017).

6. Barbara Miner, "Ultimate $uperpower: Supersized dollars drive 'Waiting for "Superman"' agenda," Not Waiting for Superman, 2010 (available at: http://www.notwaitingforsuperman.org/Articles/20101020-MinerUltimate Superpower/, accessed May 10, 2017).

7. Ibid.

8. See, for example, Hedgeclippers, "Hedgepapers No. 10—The double standard of success academy," April 20, 2015 (available at: http://hedgeclippers.org/hedgepaper-10-the-double-standard-of-success-academy/, accessed May 3, 2017); Joanne Barkan, "Got dough? How billionaires rule our schools," *Dissent*, winter 2011 (available at: https://www.dissentmagazine.org/article/got-dough-how-billionaires-rule-our-schools/, accessed September 1, 2017).

9. Sarah Reckhow, *Follow the Money: How Foundation Dollars Change Public School Politics*, Oxford: Oxford University Press, 2013.

10. Ravitch, *Reign of Error*.

11. Quoted from "Current research," Center for Reinventing Public Education, April 21, 2017 (available at: http://www.crpe.org/current-research/, accessed May 5, 2017).

12. Quoted from "Experts," Center for Reinventing Public Education, (available at: http://www.crpe.org/about-us/experts/, accessed May 25, 2017).

13. Dora Taylor, "To kill a vampire: The continued resurrection of charter schools in Washington State," *The Progressive*, September 2, 2016 (available at: http://progressive.org/public-school-shakedown/kill-vampire-continued-resurrection-charter-schools-washington-state/, accessed April 21, 2017).

14. Quoted in Linda Shaw, "Gates Foundation pours funds into education advocacy groups," *Seattle Times*, 6 August 2011 (available at: http://www.seattletimes.com/seattle-news/gates-foundation-pours-funds-into-education-advocacy-groups/, accessed September 1, 2017).

15. To get a sense of the expansion of these types of public–private ventures over recent years, see the Department of Education blog: "HomeRoom" (available at https://blog.ed.gov/2011/10/public-private-partnerships-leveraging-resources-for-student-success/, accessed May 10, 2017).

16. Ravitch, *Reign of Error*, p. 248.

17. See Erica Frankenberg, Genevieve Siegel-Hawley, and Jia Wang, "Choice without equity: Charter school segregation and the need for civil rights standards" Civil Rights Project report, January, 2010 (available at: http://escholarship.org/uc/item/4r07q8kg, accessed August 22, 2017). For a more specific recent case of re-segregation in North Carolina charter schools, see Helen Ladd, Charles Clotfelter, and John Holbein, "The Growing Segmentation of the Charter School Sector in North Carolina," CALDER Working Paper No 133, August 2015 (available at: http://www.caldercenter.org/sites/default/files/WP%20133_0.pdf, accessed August 22, 2017).

18. Rachel Cohen, "The devastating impact of school closures on students and communities," *American Prospect,* April 22, 2016 (available at: http://www. alternet.org/education/devastating-impact-school-closures-students-and-communities, accessed September 1, 2017).

19. David Harvey, *The New Imperialism,* Oxford: Oxford University Press, 2003.

20. Karl Marx, *Capital: A Critique of Political Economy,* Vol. 2, trans. Ernest Untermann, Chicago: Charles H. Kerr, 1909, p. 30.

21. From the website of BuildingBok.com. Cited in Cohen, "Devastating impact."

22. Pauline Lipman, *The New Political Economy of Urban Education: Neoliberalism, Race, and the Right to the City,* New York: Routledge, 2011.

23. Elvin Wyly, Markus Moos, Daniel Hammel, and Emmanuel Kabahizi, "Cartographies of race and class: Mapping the class-monopoly rents of American subprime mortgage capital," *International Journal of Urban and Regional Research* 33/2 (2009), pp. 332–354.

24. William Watkins, *The White Architects of Black Education,* New York: Teacher's College, 2001.

25. Banhi Bhattacharya, "Academy schools in England," *Childhood Education* 89/2 (2013), p. 95.

26. Anne West and Elizabeth Bailey, "The development of the academies programme: 'Privatising' school-based education in England, 1986–2013," *British Journal of Educational Studies* 61/2 (2013), pp. 137–159.

27. Bhattacharya, "Academy schools," p. 96.

28. The academies program was originally called City Academies. See Helen Gunter, Philip Woods, and Glenys Wood, "Researching academies in England," *Management in Education* 22/4 (2008), p. 3.

29. "'City academies' to tackle school failure," *BBC News,* September 15, 2000 (available at: http://news.bbc.co.uk/2/hi/uk_news/education/925378.stm/, accessed May 23, 2017).

30. "Glossary," UK Department of Education (available at: http://www. education.gov.uk/edubase/glossary.xhtml/, accessed May 15, 2017).

31. West and Bailey, "Development of the academies programme," p. 144.

32. Ibid., p. 147.

33. Paul Miller, "Free choice, free schools and the academisation of education in England," *Research in Comparative and International Education* 6/2 (2011), p. 173.

34. "What does it mean to be an academy school?" *BBC News,* May 7, 2016 (available at: http://www.bbc.com/news/education-13274090, accessed May 23, 2017).

35. Stephen Gorard, "What are academies the answer to?" *Journal of Education Policy* 24/1 (2009), pp. 101–113.

36. Javier Espinoza, "'Academy chains' performance 'less impressive' than local authorities, new ranking shows," *Daily Telegraph,* July 7, 2016 (available at: http://www.telegraph.co.uk/education/2016/07/06/academy-chains-performance-less-impressive-than-local-authorities/, accessed May 25, 2017).

37. Tania Branigan, "Top school's creationists preach value of biblical story over evolution," *Guardian*, March 8, 2002 (available at: https://www.theguardian.com/uk/2002/mar/09/schools.religion, accessed May 23, 2017).

38. Philip Woods, Glenys Woods, and Helen Gunter, "Academy schools and entrepreneurialism in education," *Journal of Education Policy* 22/2 (2007), p. 237.

39. Fiona Millar, "School reforms widen poverty gap, new research finds," *Guardian*, August 2, 2016 (available at: https://www.theguardian.com/education/2016/aug/02/school-widen-poverty-admissions-academy-free-schools-segregation/, accessed May 23, 2017).

40. Stephen Gorard, "The link between academies in England, pupil outcomes and local patterns of socio-economic segregation between schools," *Research Papers in Education* 29/3 (2014), pp. 268–284.

41. Daniel Boffey and Warwick Mansell, "Are England's academies being a cash cow for business?" *Guardian*, June 12, 2016 (available at: https://www.theguardian.com/education/2016/jun/12/academy-schools-cash-cow-business/, accessed May 23, 2017).

42. See, for example, some of the new policies in British Columbia enabling the emergence of private sources of revenue as discussed in Wendy Poole and Gerald Fallon, "The emerging fourth tier in K-12 education finance in British Columbia, Canada: Increasing privatisation and implications for social justice," *Globalisation, Societies and Education* 13/3 (2015), pp. 339–368.

Chapter 8

1. See Louis Althusser, *On the Reproduction of Capitalism: Ideology and Ideological State Apparatuses*, London: Verso, 2014.

2. Katharyne Mitchell, Sallie Marston, and Cindi Katz, *Life's Work: Geographies of Social Reproduction*, Oxford: Blackwell, 2004.

3. Elspeth Probyn, "The spatial imperative of subjectivity," in Kay Anderson, Mona Domosh, Steve Pile, and Nigel Thrift (eds), *Handbook of Cultural Geography*, London: Sage, 2003, p. 290–299.

4. Ibid., p. 298.

5. Mary Thomas, "'I think it's just natural': The spatiality of racial segregation at a US high school," *Environment and Planning A* 37/7 (2005), p. 1234.

6. Teresa de Lauretis, *Technologies of Gender: Essays on Theory, Film and Fiction*, Bloomington: Indiana University Press, 1988.

7. Jouni Häkli and Kirsi Kallio, "The global as a field: Children's rights advocacy as a transnational practice," *Environment and Planning D: Society and Space* 32/2 (2014), pp. 293–309.

8. See the blog of Sue Peters, Dora Taylor, and Carolyn Leith (available at https://seattleeducation2010.wordpress.com/about/, accessed April 27, 2017).

9. Quoted from "About PAA," Parents Across America (available at http://parentsacrossamerica.org/who-we-are/, accessed April 27, 2017).

10. Sue Peters and Dora Taylor, "About us," Seattle Education 2010 (available at: https://seattleeducation2010.wordpress.com/about/, accessed April 27, 2017).

11. Jesse Hagopian, *More than a Score: The New Uprising Against High-Stakes Testing*, Chicago: Haymarket Press, 2014.

12. Cited in Laura Flanders, "The fight against high-stakes testing: A civil rights movement," *Truthout*, March 31, 2015 (available at: http://www.truth-out.org/progressivepicks/item/29948-is-the-next-civil-rights-movement-against-high-stakes-tests/, accessed September 1, 2017).

13. See "Who We Are," Journey for Justice Alliance (available at: https://www.j4jalliance.com/aboutj4j/, accessed April 27, 2017).

14. Ibid.

15. We were aided on the project by our graduate research assistants Ryan Burns and Elyse Gordon.

16. New geospatial technologies allow educators to teach these types of collaborative experiential skills through the use of participatory GIS and other web-based mapping tools. These types of tools and skills can enable groups of participants to explore and discuss together the implications of specific decisions affecting their spatial surroundings.

17. Brian Harley, "Deconstructing the map," *Cartographica* 26/2 (1989), p. 429.

18. Rob Fiedler, Nadine Schuurman, and Jennifer Hyndman, "Hidden homelessness in greater Vancouver," *Cities* 23/3 (2006), pp. 205–216.

19. William Tate and Mark Hogrebe, "From visuals to vision: Using GIS to inform civic dialogue about African American males," *Race, Ethnicity and Education* 14/1 (2011), pp. 51–71.

20. James Blaut, George McCleary, and América Blaut, "Environmental mapping in young children," *Environment and Behavior* 2 (1970), pp. 335–349.

21. Jean Piaget and Bärbel Inhelder, *The Child's Conception of Space*, London: Routledge, 1956.

22. Lev Vygotsky, *Thought and Language*, Cambridge, MA: MIT Press, 1962.

23. These insights were carried forward primarily by Patrick Wiegand vis-à-vis the connections between collaborative learning and improved spatial cognition. See his book *Learning and Teaching with Maps*, London: Routledge, 2006.

24. Kristen Buras, "'We have to tell our story': Neo-griots, racial resistance, and schooling in the other South," *Race, Ethnicity and Education* 12/4 (2009), pp. 427–453.

Chapter 9

1. Bernard Stiegler, *Technics and Time 1: The Fault of Epimetheus*, trans. Richard Beardsworth and George Collins, Stanford: Stanford University Press, 1998; *Technics and Time 2: Disorientation*, trans. S. Barker, Stanford: Stanford University Press, 2009.

2. The research was conducted in collaboration with Sarah Elwood and with the help of research assistants Ryan Burns, Elyse Gordon, and Tricia Ruiz.

3. Richard Hugo, "Duwamish head," *Making Certain it Goes On: The Collected Poems of Richard Hugo*, New York: Norton, 1991, pp. 65–68.
4. Notably, some students transferred these insights directly into their daily lives. At an event where the students shared their science/history project with parents, one mother reported to us that her daughter had recently insisted the family begin using biodegradable soap.
5. See Maurizio Lazzarato, *Signs and Machines: Capitalism and the Production of Subjectivity*, Cambridge, MA: MIT Press, 2014.

Index

Treaty of Amsterdam, 74
Trump, Donald, 16–17, 22, 127
tuition, 19, 40–1, 73, 146

uneven development, 5–6, 8, 14, 16,
    27, 110, 145, 163
uniforms, 89, 91–2, 116–17
United Nations Educational, Scientific
    and Cultural Organization
    (UNESCO), 67, 70
Universal Declaration of Human
    Rights, 69
Universities, 19–20, 40–2, 64, 118,
    125–6, 133, 135
University of Washington, 5, 125
US Department of Education, 125, 127
US Environmental Protection Agency,
    158

value, 3–4, 10, 13, 24–7, 29, 31, 33,
    35–6, 42, 59, 61, 65, 70, 73–4,

78–80, 83, 89, 99, 102–3, 112,
    114, 126, 134, 140, 163
Vancouver, 49, 83, 88, 96,
    Richmond, 83, 88–96
Vardy Foundation, 133–4
Vygotsky, Lev, 149

Walden Media, 121
Walt Disney Company, 35
Walton Family Foundation, 99, 111,
    122–3, 125
Walton, Sam, 126
Washington, DC, 101, 122, 128
Watkins, William, 131
welfare, 13–14, 21, 32, 53, 71, 73, 84
white flight, 17, 19
whiteness, 59
Willis, Paul, 3, 47
World Trade Organization (WTO), 15
World War II, 13, 17, 28, 48, 56, 150,
    153